Marketing for Nonmarketers

Marketing for Nonmarketers

Principles & Tactics
That Everyone in
Business Must Know

Houston G. Elam
Norton Paley

amacom
American Management Association

This publication is designed to provide accurate and authoritative information in regard to the subject matter covered. It is sold with the understanding that the publisher is not engaged in rendering legal, accounting, or other professional service. If legal advice or other expert assistance is required, the services of a competent professional person should be sought.

658.8
E371ma

Library of Congress Cataloging-in-Publication Data

Elam, Houston G.
    Marketing for Nonmarketers / Houston G. Elam, Norton
    Paley.
        p.   cm.
    Includes index.
    ISBN 0-8144-5993-5
    1. Marketing.   I. Paley, Norton.   II. Title.
    HF5415.E49   1992
    658.8—dc20   91-41985
                                                         CIP

Printing number

10   9   8   7   6   5   4   3   2   1

This book is dedicated to:

Beth and *Doug Elam*

Annette Paley
and to *Susan, Julia,* and *Gordon*

Contents

Preface

This is a book about marketing written for executives and professionals whose job function is *not* marketing. Its purpose is to explain and illustrate what marketing is all about, what marketing professionals do, what roles nonmarketers play, and how marketing functions within the corporate structure.

There could hardly be a better time for achieving an understanding of marketing's importance. International tariff barriers are falling. Large U.S. companies are making marketing agreements with businesses in other countries and consolidating their positions in this country. Foreign companies are aggressively challenging U.S. companies at home and overseas. Truly global marketing strategies are developing, and competition has never been more fierce.

With technology and research creativity resulting in enormous numbers of new products, the corporate focus has shifted to achieving profitability through effective sales—sales at a profit. This goal can be accomplished only through effective marketing. If you read on, you will learn why:

- As a nonmarketing executive you will benefit in your own position if you understand marketing better and learn more about the skills marketers need to do their jobs.
- As a finance executive, you will profit from knowing more about marketing because you will understand and maybe even appreciate many of the budgets and expenditures related to that function.
- As a production manager, you will come to have a clearer picture of the marketing situation and why some of the best products are dropped and replaced by others. You will also appreciate why the company seems to be unsure of what products it

ix

really wants to make, even though it has a strong tradition in a particular field.

- As an accountant, you'll understand the necessity for travel expenses incurred by marketing executives and why marketers operate under different rules from most other managers.
- As a member of the research staff, you will learn that marketers use the same scientific methods you use, applying them to marketing issues. You will learn that marketers also plan far more than you may now believe. Indeed, most of what appears to be last-minute activity is actually planned in advance to look that way. In this book, we will try to explain why.

The book raises and answers a number of basic questions, from what marketing is to what marketers do. It considers issues such as: Is marketing based on a theory or just luck? How much of marketing expenses is really necessary? Do marketing professionals really know what they are doing? Why is there such a difference between the production price and the selling price of so many products?

This book is written with the nonmarketing manager in mind and uses terms and concepts familiar to all. Many examples are provided to clarify tactics and approaches. Material is presented in several different ways to ensure that it is understood. Numerous case examples permit the reader to consider a situation prior to learning what the company actually did. We hope and believe that we have provided essential information and made it interesting to read.

Portions of this text originally appeared in our earlier book, *Marketing for the Non-Marketing Executive* (AMACOM 1978). In the present volume we have dealt with critical current issues and, of course, have updated both terminology and examples. We have structured the material so that each chapter can stand alone and be read separately with only minimal loss to the reader, making it easier for the reader to skip around. In order to facilitate this approach, we have included a short review of some material at the start of several chapters. So if something seems familiar from an earlier section of the book, keep reading for a moment and you should find yourself in new territory.

ORGANIZATION OF THE BOOK

A study of any complex subject matter requires some direction. Because the material discussed in this book is aimed at nonmarketing managers in industry, we use the general framework of planning and implementation, activities common to managers in any specialization. The approach covers familiar territory but gives special emphasis to subjects such as collecting and analyzing data, setting policy and establishing objectives, planning, and making and implementing decisions, each from the perspective of the marketing manager or the marketing function.

We focus on two different perspectives of marketing activity: (1) individual product market targets and corporate issues, sometimes called "micromarketing" issues; and (2) industry, national, and international issues related to marketing policies, sometimes called "macromarketing."

Chapter 1 provides an overview of marketing, defining it and placing the marketing executive's role in perspective. The key role played by the executive team, especially given the realities of the new global market, is explored.

Chapter 2 traces some of the transitions of the marketing function over time, focusing on the concept of consumer satisfaction and providing an up-to-date analysis of the changing international marketing environment.

Chapter 3 discusses the broad spectrum of data—internal and external, primary and secondary, directly and indirectly collected, economic, competitive, social, political, and emotional response—that are part of the marketing intelligence essential to create an effective strategic marketing plan for achieving a competitive edge.

Chapter 4 describes the organization and tools of analysis typically used by marketers. These tools may be performance measurements in various areas of the operation or financial checks, such as determining return on investment or a company's break-even point. The results of the analyses are then used as guides in forecasting and budgeting, the prerequisites for preparing any strategic marketing plan.

Chapter 5 uses criteria from the behavioral sciences to analyze the pressures and influences on consumers—why they react to some products and presentations and not others and what can be done to improve a company's chances for success in a given situation.

Chapter 6 discusses the job of planning in a dynamic market-focused organization. It describes the benefits of planning, presents an outline of a long-term strategic marketing plan, and illustrates the use of multifunctional management teams in an organized planning process.

Chapter 7 focuses on the short-term tactical marketing plan that becomes the basis of marketing action once the policy issues described in Chapters 1–6 have been determined.

Chapter 8 focuses on turning strategic plans into operating strategy. It comments on those factors a company can and cannot control and on how the marketing manager should adjust a strategy accordingly. Several levels of strategy are presented, as are elements of effective strategy development.

Chapter 9 pulls together all the concepts presented throughout the book, illustrating the action steps that result in the strong marketing logic essential for the company's success.

ACKNOWLEDGMENTS

As is true of all such projects, we owe a debt to many. First of all, we must acknowledge the suggestions sent to us from readers of the first edition. Their thoughtfulness has been helpful in many ways. Also, we want to thank Adrienne Hickey, senior acquisitions and planning editor, AMACOM Books, for her encouragement and support, and Jacqueline Laks Gorman for her editorial insights and guidance. We want to thank Nancy Reubert for her accurate transcription of materials. Thanks also to Susan Paley for her pragmatic review of major chapters and to Beth Elam for her assistance in resolving organizational problems. Last but not least, we want to acknowledge the fact that a number of the examples in the book have appeared in Norton Paley's column in *Monday Morning Marketing Memo*, published monthly by the American Management Association. Without that constant pressure to remain current, this book would not have the benefit of such rich practical content.

H.G.E.
N.P.

PART ONE

Clarifying the Marketing Role

CHAPTER 1

Marketing:
The Competitive
Function of the Company

The dramatic change occurring in the world economic environment—so dramatic, in fact, that most of it would not have been predicted even several years ago—has placed marketing in the position of corporate hero or villain. Reflect on the following events:

- The global market is now a reality, as is the existence of truly international and multinational corporations.
- The European Community (EC) is removing internal trade barriers, creating the largest and richest single market in the world.
- Eastern Europe is becoming a battlefield as corporations compete for dominance in thousands of product areas.
- The new coordinated North American Free Trade Zone has altered the way business is conducted on the North American continent by establishing a single marketplace across Canadian and U.S. borders, and perhaps in Mexico as well.
- The importance of the nations of the Pacific Rim as both producers and consumers continues to grow.
- As market internationalization increases, companies in all countries are seeking new markets for their products and are facing increasing product intrusion by others into their own traditional markets.

3

In each of these cases, competition will be brutal, tactics will be dramatic, and actions and counteractions will have to be swift and effective. And, in every case, *marketing* will become the focal point for the growth and survival of the companies involved.

What better time for nonmarketing executives to become more familiar with the many aspects of marketing and the marketing manager's job? By taking this step, you will become more aware of how and why marketers do what they do and be in a better position to intelligently influence some of those decisions to the benefit of your company. Acquiring that familiarity is what this book is all about. We consider it essential that management at all levels work together, which can occur only if all those involved understand the role of others on the team.

Unlike most economic opportunities, the time for effective initial access to the opening markets we have noted will be short. The companies that enter the new markets early and are able to make an impact will have what amounts to "squatters' rights" against later arrivals. Such rights will not save an inefficient competitor but will provide some advantages that can be used effectively by strong companies against latecomers.

Our stress on international markets does not diminish the importance of domestic markets. Rather, it is intended to emphasize how domestic markets will themselves continue to become more competitive as a result of easier corporate entry. Few markets are safe from aggressive new product entry now, and this trend should continue for the foreseeable future.

All this change is occurring in an environment in which new products are entering the marketplace at breakneck speeds, altering and replacing existing products in the process. Who would have believed, a few years ago, that FAX machines, laptop PCs with modems, air phones, or computerized vest pocket reminders would rapidly become the tools of everyday management operations?

THE MARKETING EXECUTIVE'S FUNCTION

As you will learn, the functions performed by marketing executives influence decisions in every area of the organization. Decisions on products, promotions, styles, shapes, colors, smells, sizes, and slogans are all part of the marketing executive's carefully planned approach. The marketing of every item is complex in its own right. Distribution of products represents a case in point; consider how complex a task it is to distribute bars of candy to 40,000 outlets around the country and come out ahead financially, especially if each candy bar is sold for less than half a dollar.

In this book we discuss questions such as: Does the marketer know what the customer really wants? Is there a system to marketing, or does it really come down to luck? Are there reasons for the many iffy decisions being made in the marketing area? Are they based on a special logic, theory, or process? The answer to each of these questions is yes. There are theories that apply, and there are sound and strong reasons for the approaches used. Knowledge of the facts and theories will be invaluable to you, the nonmarketing manager, as you try to get some perspective on the role of the marketer in your organization. Furthermore, it will enhance the way you function in your own role, which is mutually dependent with marketing.

Questions Nonmarketers Ask About the Marketing Role

Let's start by putting on the table some of the questions nonmarketers typically ask about marketing.

Production Management Questions

- Why do so many different products continue to be manufactured when some don't seem to sell well at all?
- Why are some of the best products eliminated from production, while other, less efficient models go right on selling?
- Why does a company with a traditional strong suit continue to experiment and branch out into new product areas in which they fail, only to try again in another area?
- Why can't we establish a predictable relationship between price and cost?
- Why are some of the very best test products abandoned?

Financial Management Questions

- Why is so much money—often in excess of 50 percent of a product's total cost—spent on promotion and distribution?
- Why not use independent distribution systems instead of our own facilities to shift the payment dates forward and eliminate a substantial area of seemingly unnecessary costs?

- Why are there so many virtually identical products, and why are products priced lower if we make them and sell them under "private" labels?
- Why don't we schedule our production more evenly over the year and save a substantial amount of money?
- Why don't we send more of our supply needs out for bids and save substantial amounts of money instead of continuing to contract with a limited number of suppliers?
- Why don't we use tighter credit policies?
- Why do so many marketing people have such large expense accounts?

Headquarters Staff Questions

- Why does the marketing group continue to use outside firms and consultants in such areas as advertising and marketing research when such services could be provided much less expensively from within the company?
- Why is there so much controversy concerning deceptive advertising practices?
- Why are so many marketing decisions made so quickly, when a little more research and study would seem in order?
- Since we already have a strong product mix, why don't we spend less money on marketing intelligence and product development and pass the savings along to stockholders?
- Why does there appear to be so much more debate during the decision process in the marketing area than in other areas of the organization?
- Whose decision was it to advertise on that terrible TV show that nobody likes, instead of the top-rated show competing against it on another channel?

Each of these questions probably has a good, strong, and defensible answer from the marketing standpoint, and each is important to the long-term interests of the company.

MARKETING AND OTHERS ON THE MANAGEMENT TEAM

Because management must work as a team, it is helpful for managers to recognize the point of view, as well as the needs and requirements, of the other executives within the management unit. Only then can individual managers begin to understand why certain questions that seem so unimportant from one side of the table are given great weight on the other side. To the marketer, issues such as ensuring the shortest possible delivery time and providing error-free high-quality products represent far more than maintaining standards—they mean a loss or gain of sales.

Similarly, to the marketer, pricing is more than cost. It is a variable to be used actively and changed freely as part of a careful strategy for increasing profits. Sometimes a price position works as a fulcrum to bring about a desired short-term drop in sales or profits in order to accomplish a larger objective for future advantage. Each of these cases requires a marketing decision to complete the cycle, for without profitable sales from identified customers, all is lost.

On the other hand, the marketing executive is at the mercy of a faulty production schedule, insufficient funding, or records that do not contain the information necessary to identify potential markets or customers. Mutual dependence works both ways.

MARKETING DEFINED

> Marketing is a total system of interacting business activities designed to plan, price, promote, and distribute want-satisfying products and services to organizational and household users at a profit in a competitive environment.

It is important to view marketing as a systemic philosophy and approach to doing business. It is equally important to recognize that marketing requires interacting business activities, reinforcing the premise that each area of management has a stake in the successful operation of the company and depends on every other area if it is to do its part properly.

Recognizing that marketers expect to be in a state of competitive readiness is consistent with our definition, as is the inference that marketers operate in much the same way as military strategists— effective marketing must be carefully thought out and thoroughly orchestrated as it is being carried out.

The need to provide want-satisfying products and services seems at first to be obvious; products wanted by customers are the ones the company should be offering for sale. Behind the obvious, however, are several eminently more complex issues, which will become major discussion points in Chapter 2.

Our definition stresses profit-making and competition, terms which do not fit neatly into the roles of nonprofit organizations or governmental agencies. Does this imply that they do not perform the marketing function? The answer is no. It does mean, however, that such organizations use many of the techniques of marketing and adopt the marketing philosophy of customer service, modified to meet their objectives. Such organizations and agencies are not the major focus of this book and are discussed only when such illustrations assist all managers to understand an important point.

You may wish to skip ahead and look at marketing's dynamic side, exploring the types of strategic theory essential to the function, before learning about the intelligence-gathering and tools-of-analysis aspects of the job. This approach may make the experience more dramatic and give you a better angle on the environment and process issues.

Whether you choose to look at the subject this way or to proceed in order through the book, once you are on the trail of marketing activities and responsibilities you will doubtless find yourself fascinated by the problems and opportunities they present; you will also have a clearer insight into why and how marketers do the things they do. You may discover new ways to improve total performance. At least you will know the right questions to ask in determining where things are going wrong.

CHAPTER 2

Marketers — Catalysts for Change

How important are new products to the current economy? Consider this statistic—well over half of the products now in use have been developed within the last forty years. Look around your house. All the kitchen appliances, from dishwasher to coffee maker, are new, as are all the home entertainment systems and even most of the lawn equipment. In the typical office, only the furniture and metal file cabinets may have been around as long as ten years. None of the electronic communications items, none of the current computers, not even the collating two-sided color copiers existed then; there may, however, still be a few old IBM Selectric typewriters, the wonder product of the 1960s.

In virtually every area of the economy, the same is true—new products are appearing and being replaced at a seemingly ever faster rate. Today's marketplace is both hectic and customer-dominated. The management of marketing activities within that marketplace has become an increasingly important task.

THE VITALITY OF CAPITALISM

Before proceeding with our discussion of change, let us pause for a moment and place several basic ideas in some perspective so that we can proceed with an understanding of how we reached this point of ever-present change.

The U.S. business system operates on the assumption that people—and therefore companies—perform best when they know that good performance benefits them directly. If a company finds that a competitor has introduced a new product similar to one it already has on the market, priced about the same but of superior quality, the company will have to find ways of improving its own product; otherwise, it will suffer a drop in sales and profits. When the first company improves its own product, the competition has the marketing disadvantage; it will then be that competing company's turn to find a way to make its own product appear more valuable to the consumer. This is what Adam Smith meant when he wrote that all of capitalist society benefits through the "hidden hand" of individuals seeking personal gain in markets. The capitalist system encourages continuing product improvement within a market, a cycle of action and reaction to major changes in competition, each move opening up the possibility of new expectations of benefits for the consumer.

The stronger the competitive structure, the greater the pressure on the marketing executive. So successful have U.S. marketing techniques been that the last three decades have prompted a tremendous effort on the part of most other countries, socialist and capitalist alike, to copy them.

It is instructive to note that while the Japanese stress on quality has received appropriate international attention, at least as important has been their effort to emulate the U.S. marketing approach. This latter effort is a cornerstone of Japan's economic success, validating the importance of the role of marketing both today and in the coming years.

THE EVOLUTION OF THE U.S. MARKETING ECONOMY

Coordinated marketing management as a formal activity emerged as the subject of serious study in the early 1950s, although a number of U.S. companies had already worked out their own systems and procedures before that. With such companies as General Electric, International Business Machines, General Motors, Eastman Kodak, and Procter & Gamble leading the way, formal marketing structures were gradually adopted by top management of most companies.

To make the most effective use of marketing, it is helpful to understand the relationship between new technology and the pace of change in the marketplace, how the forces of environment and change affect each other, how profit influences planning, why the concept of marketing has become so important, what the detailed benefits of planning are, and how to organize for efficient marketing.

The Rate of Change and the Growth of Technology

While change itself may be an ever-present characteristic of the U.S. marketplace, the pace at which it occurs can and does vary. The rate of change has been increasing steadily since the days of the Industrial Revolution. At first, change came relatively slowly, but since World War II, it has been accelerating head over heels.

Every major change has resulted in a different consumer response in the marketplace, a different competitive situation. To be successful, a marketer has to anticipate and prepare for change, not just respond to it. Therefore, the more rapidly change takes place, the more vital the need for quick, accurate anticipation and adaptation.

There is a direct relationship between production technology and the rate of change within an economy. As technology improves, the pace of change quickens. The roots of modern production technology, and thus the story of marketing in the United States, began with the Industrial Revolution of the late 1700s and early 1800s. The development of improved production technology continued into the 1900s.

Typically, manufacturers during this period were able to sell most products made, but production was not yet able to keep up with demand. Over decades, as more people began working in industry or offices and earning more money each year, they became able to purchase more products to improve their standard of living, resulting in ever-greater demand for more products. All of this changed during the 1930s when, for a period of ten years, the economy came almost to a standstill.

The Depression: A Switch in Market Emphasis. Depressions had occurred before, but the depression of the 1930s was especially damaging. From a marketing point of view, the problem was not only trying to find ways to mend the economy as a whole but the need to compete with every other marketer in wooing those few-and-far-between customers who had any buying power left.

Production during the depression was still planned according to what manufacturers thought they could turn out most profitably, but more emphasis was placed on post-production activities, including marketing. Advertising and sales promotion were designed to influence customers to buy this product or that one. By the end of the depression, promotion had become so important that large ads were common in newspapers and magazines and radio commercials bubbled with jingles and snappy one-liners.

The Growing Consumer Market After World War II. World War II cured the last symptoms of the depression. With labor and materials concentrated on the war effort, essential products and luxury products alike were in short supply. Innovation and substitution became a way of life during the war, making the early to mid 1940s what many consider the Second Industrial Revolution. New methods of food preparation and packaging opened up the old can of peas and introduced the new frozen product. New building materials included aluminum, glass, plastics, and concrete, replacing the iron, steel, and wood needed for war supplies. Among the many synthetic products that were developed, substitutes for rubber and butter took a permanent place in the postwar marketplace.

After World War II, the production lines reverted to producing consumer products. The business picture looked bright. People were eager to see many consumer products that had either been very scarce or even impossible to find during the war. Consumers also had the money to spend. Those who had been in the armed forces or who had worked in the factories had saved much of what they had earned, having had so little available to spend it on during the war, and they wanted to go out and splurge.

To many manufacturers, planning seemed a simple matter. All they needed to do, they thought, was to identify a good product, tool up for its production, turn the machines on, and produce that product for years and years. What they overlooked was how drastically the country's production capability had changed. The mass production techniques picked up during the war had given manufacturers the ability to produce many more products much more quickly than ever before. Production engineers had of necessity learned how to innovate, substitute, and redesign equipment with imagination and speed during the war. The result: a marketplace flooded with products and stronger competition than ever before.

The 1950s: The Glutted Marketplace. Because postwar business planning focused so strongly on the production line and all but ignored changes in customer demand, what was considered an almost endless potential market in the late 1940s became oversupplied in the early 1950s. Here are three examples of potential sales slumps narrowly avoided by innovative thinking:

1. In 1946, automobile manufacturers began producing the first cars to come off the line since early 1942. People were eager for new cars. So successfully did the industry satisfy that hunger, however, that by the early 1950s there was a slump in sales. The market had been saturated. To counteract the trend, automobile manufacturers created a new line of personalized cars.

2. Before the war, iceboxes were far more common than refrigerators, automatic clothes washers and dryers were a novelty, and the home freezer was almost nonexistent. Yet by the early 1950s, the market for these appliances was so completely saturated that additional sales were achieved only through severe price-cutting. In fact, modern discount stores were first introduced to encourage the sale of large home appliances.

3. The brand-new home television market developed in the late 1940s. By 1955, the industry was in serious trouble—not because of a waning interest in television but because practically everyone already owned a set by then. Assembly lines no longer had to turn out large numbers of sets. How did TV manufacturers avoid a disastrous decline in sales? They developed and sold "second sets"—small table-top units.

Numerous similar examples could be found in virtually every segment of every market and industry.

By the 1950s, the productive capacity of manufacturers had reached the stage at which almost any market demand could be met very quickly, but marketers had not yet learned how to plan effectively. The time between the introduction of a new product and the inevitable decline of its sales—the product life cycle—had dropped from many years to just a few years (today, in some markets, it is approaching a matter of a few months), but marketers had not yet learned to forecast and adapt to these inevitable changes. Yet no company can depend for its fortune on the production of a single successful product and expect rich profits for years to come. Products— all products—go through stages of success and eventual replacement. Consider, for example, several product changes that have occurred in recent years at the office and in the home.

At the Office

- Computer word processors have replaced electric typewriters.
- Copying machines have replaced carbon paper.
- Notebook computers weighing four to six pounds are replacing the twelve-pound-and-up laptops of several years ago.
- Telephone answering machines and voice mail units have replaced switchboard answering services.
- Ballpoint pens have replaced fountain pens.

In the Home

- Compact discs are replacing audiocassettes, which replaced long-playing records.
- The Beta format videotape has been virtually replaced by the VHS format.
- Radio alarm clocks have replaced windup alarm clocks.
- Camcorders have replaced 8-mm. home movie units.
- Microwave ovens have replaced second ovens.

We will return to the subject of product life cycles in Chapter 8.

TODAY'S ROAD TO PROFIT — THE MARKETING CONCEPT

Low Costs ≠ High Profits

As a manager, you are aware of the need to provide for a healthy profit; profit tends to indicate the healthy mainstream of your activities.

Because costs are a major profit-retarding factor, it is only natural that managers focus on them as the major factor affecting profits. Many companies have built their structures in a direct response to this set of logical relationships. But it may be that the emphasis on holding down production costs constitutes the biggest problem of all, for it tends to stifle those creative activities that might reduce profits in the short run—but increase them in the long term. New and different products offer the best hope for the future.

What, then, is the real generating force behind profit? Is it selling products above cost? No doubt about it—but what counts is the *sale price,* not the *cost.* This point is far too important to be made so simply, as it tends to be overlooked. The company's goal must be to get the customer to prefer and to be willing—even eager—to buy a particular product, even at a higher price.

Not grasping this point is what undid Henry Ford. Ford had an enormously efficient production line turning out his famous Model T; he is said to have offered the car in "any color you want, so long as you want black." The car was affordable and easily fixed at home. Nevertheless, by failing to individualize his product, Ford lost the market he had created and opened up the field for others to develop cars that would compete by offering a variety of different features, sizes, shapes, and colors that fit customers' particular needs better than Ford's one-size-fits-all Model T. In essence, the other companies built their competing cars to try to reach particular groups of customers, not to reach *all* customers. By following that approach, they were able to lure customers away from Ford, even though the new models cost more; price was not the key reason for the purchases. And since the new models cost more, the new companies made a lot more money.

The approach to a successful future starts with the recognition that (1) change is inevitable, and (2) costs are by no means the only factors to consider. As we noted earlier in this chapter, marketers had quite a time keeping profits up just after World War II, not because there wasn't a strong demand for many of the new products but because the production technology gained from the war effort satisfied demand faster than manufacturers could invent new products to offer an avid public. The problem was further compounded by the fact that product life cycles were getting shorter; even if a company found a product with a strong market position, it could no longer count on a long, successful job run for continued profit. Marketers who had previously calculated profits on how many units they would run off the production line could no longer assume that just because an existing product or product assortment was profitable one year, it was guaranteed of doing equally well the next. The new technology created the need for a new system of planning for profit.

The Production Orientation

In its simplest form, *production orientation* allowed a company to manufacture those new products its production line could manufacture most efficiently and profitably. Historically, this approach kept costs down because the only new products that were added to a company's line were those that the company's machinery and labor force could produce with little need for retooling or retraining.

Production orientation emphasized the manufacture of products at their lowest cost (usually passing the savings on to the customer as a competitive weapon), making production experts the most influential managers in the company. And what could be more sensible than making maximum use of existing facilities?

However, the production approach gradually crippled companies that sought to continue making profits in the changing marketing climate. As we know, profit is not related to production cost alone; it also depends on the marketability of the product. In a highly competitive marketplace, only those products that please customers win sales—and profits.

Eventually, the production-oriented approach resulted in a profit dive, because it neglected what should have been a prime concern—the customer. We do not mean to say that costs are unimportant, for indeed they are. But costs are relative to opportunity. High production costs by themselves should not eliminate further consideration of a particular product—if there is a strong possibility that the product will return ample profits.

The Market Orientation

By the 1960s top management realized that the days of planning profits based on production needs were over. Managers were going to have to research what customers wanted and then figure out how to give it to them.

This new way to plan for profit—labeled the *marketing concept*—is geared to the wants and needs of the consumer. A company that uses the marketing concept works out a profitable product development plan, systematically developing products within a particular area. It means that a company studies consumer habits and attitudes and tests its ideas before putting products on the market. And it means that planning, both in action and in reaction to a market opportunity, must be a never-ending job. Table 2-1 compares the marketing orientation with production orientation.

The marketing concept can be used to develop a profitable product line through two channels: A company can develop a new product or it can diversify existing products or services to meet market conditions.

Table 2-1. Marketing vs. production orientation.

BUSINESS FACTOR	COMPANY'S PROBABLE EMPHASIS	
	MARKETING	PRODUCTION
Corporate attitude	Focus on consumer priorities	Focus on company priorities
Research	Market-based	Technically based
Product development	Market-based	Technically based
Product mix	Ever changing line	Limited line
Packaging	To enhance sales	To provide product durability
Sales force	To sell and bring back information	To sell existing products

New Products. New-product development involves choosing a product idea that appears to meet a customer need or want, analyzing its costs and revenues, developing it, testing it both in the laboratory and under actual market conditions, and, if the tests prove successful, introducing it to the marketplace. Careful planning gives the product a good chance of returning a respectable profit to the company.

The market orientation shapes product development more than the production orientation does. The market orientation requires a great deal of initial research, which in many cases shows that it would be better not to introduce the product at all. Still, those products that do pass all the tests have a far better chance of being just what the public needs or wants and producing strong, healthy profits for the company.

Diversification. In addition to the systematic, planned development of new products, the marketing concept presupposes an open mind to all kinds of marketing opportunities. If tests show that an entry is likely to be profitable, a marketer may even consider diversifying his or her product assortment by entering a market in which the company has had no previous experience.

Perhaps the largest single problem faced by companies interested in diversification is that many of their executives have come up through the managerial ranks and have handled only the product of a particular market. Because of their relatively narrow experience, they tend to be locked into thinking only of that market. With this type of myopic vision, many possible opportunities are never noticed simply because they do not seem to fit neatly into the company's pattern of activities to date.

An example of such myopic vision was shown by the U.S. Postal Service, which decided that sorting and delivering the mail deserved higher priority than providing a premium-priced quicker mail service. This decision enabled Federal Express to lead the way to the establishment of an entire new rapid-mail-and-package industry. Railroad executives demonstrated a similar narrow vision; they at first considered their role to be running trains of loaded freight cars *on time*. Once they realized that the real issue was movement of merchandise, they began to offer piggyback shipping—carrying truckloads of cargo on railroad cars and railroad carloads of cargo on ships.

Seizing the Opportunity

Recognizing opportunity is not as easy as it might at first seem. Nevertheless, companies that do see and seize it can benefit in dramatic ways. We offer two examples here; many others are given throughout the book.

Example 1

The Problem:

How to find a way of entering the profitable but overexposed consumer credit card market.

The Solution:

Isolate a highly desired feature not offered by any other card, at a particularly attractive price, and market it through a company that is trusted by the consumer.

The Product:

AT&T introduced the Universal Credit Card, a full-range Visa or MasterCard including telephone calling card privileges at a rate

10 percent below calling card prices, with no annual fee for life to those who applied during the first several months after the introduction of the card. Four million customers signed up, making AT&T an important competitor within six months of its entry into the industry.

Example 2

The Problem:

As the capability of VCRs expanded, programming them to record "time-shift" programs—taping movies or sports aired at inconvenient times to be available for later viewing—became ever more complicated. Manufacturers spent significant funds attempting to simplify the programming process. They developed bar codes, multiple-screen menus, laminated color-coded instruction cards, and various other approaches to simplifying programming, the key to happy VCR use. The result was broad confusion and many jokes about parents forced to pay their children to program the units for them.

The Solution:

Develop a short, standardized, easy-to-use coding system, compatible with all VCRs, that allows a viewer to program the VCR to record a program without having to determine the day, time, channel, and length of the desired show.

The Product:

VCR Plus, manufactured by Gemstar Development Corporation, is a small computerized remote unit that uses a five- or six-digit code to transmit the necessary signals to VCRs for programming.

The Initial Strategy:

Exclusive area rights to the use of the VCR Plus code were first sold to more than one hundred newspapers, including such media giants as the *New York Times*, the *Los Angeles Times*, and several regional editions of *TV Guide*. VCR Plus remote control units were introduced into several markets during the 1990 Thanksgiving weekend at $60 a unit. Although that Christmas selling season was one of the weakest in many years, with the United States in a severe recession, the units sold briskly. Projected first year sales of 1 million units were raised to perhaps 4 million units. So short was the supply that major retailers were rationing their distribution so most stores could have at least an occasional partial supply on hand.

The Future Strategy:

Gemstar Development, which is seeking patent protection for its coding technology system, is hoping to convince VCR manufacturers to build VCR Plus technology into their products. While such a setup could cost Gemstar some remote unit sales, it expects its royalty business to increase.

The marketing manager is surely key within an organization and will remain so for some time to come as new technology continues to spin out new products and saturate entire markets at a speed even greater than before. Furthermore, marketing management is, and should be, responsible for identifying, recognizing, and assisting the company in developing new products and then overseeing their successful introduction and profitable sale in an ever more competitive atmosphere.

Organizational Focus Using the Marketing Concept

The organizational structure typically found in the market-oriented company brings together the functions of sales, advertising, market research, logistics and storage, sales services, and product planning. It also creates new working relationships between marketing and the other business functions, including production, finance, and personnel.

The dramatic difference between this form of organization and that found in production-oriented companies can be seen in Figure 2-1. Note that functions that formerly were grouped under areas such as finance, engineering and research, and, particularly, production, are now part of or closely tied to the marketing function. For example, forecasting, product planning, product service, warehousing, and advertising, which are separate groups in the production-oriented company, are more integrated in the marketing-oriented company.

A marketing orientation requires that some services be shifted and recast with a split personality (part of a department shifts while part of it stays where it was). For example, engineering may retain

Figure 2-1. Shift in functional organization under marketing concept.

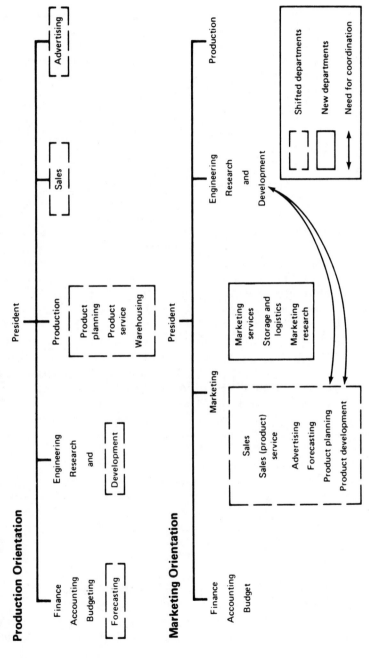

Production Orientation

President

Finance
Accounting
Budgeting
Forecasting

Engineering
Research
and
Development

Production
Product planning
Product service
Warehousing

Sales

Advertising

Marketing Orientation

President

Finance
Accounting
Budget

Marketing

Sales
Sales (product) service
Advertising
Forecasting
Product planning
Product development

Marketing services
Storage and logistics
Marketing research

Engineering
Research
and
Development

Production

Shifted departments

New departments

Need for coordination

part of product development, while another part—for example, the design of the product or its packaging—shifts to marketing. In addition, new functions, such as marketing research and marketing services, are created, giving engineers the benefit of anticipated consumer preferences prior to the completion of a product design. In a similar manner, marketers can learn about the potential of a new material or technology quicker and participate in determining how it might effectively be used.

The resulting shifts redirect the focus of central management and of the corporate decision process. The move to a marketing orientation has allowed many companies to reshape their attitudes toward their business objectives and to undertake many new ventures that would have seemed inconceivable only a short time ago.

In essence, the structure points out that marketers and nonmarketers alike play important mutually supportive roles within the corporation. Each specialist must understand the needs of other parts of the company in order to do his or her own job well, and all must work together, each person using his or her own particularly special knowledge to achieve the maximum advantage for the company as a whole. Both the shifting of roles toward marketing and the expectation that nonmarketers have knowledge valuable for marketing are important new shifts of focus and philosophy for most companies.

Another indication of widespread organizational restructuring coincident with the increasing impact of marketers within the company is the increasing flattening of corporate management hierarchies, cutting out many layers of middle management and decentralizing into product or geographic divisions or subsidiaries. This change significantly increases communication among various functional areas. Many companies, for example, have established multifunctional teams in which marketers and nonmarketers work jointly on research, intelligence gathering, and related planning projects, bringing varied perspectives to bear within a structured format. Such changes are assumed to provide closer contact between the different functional managers participating in a decision, while bringing the entire unit closer to its market and leading to better and quicker decision making.

THE DEVELOPING WORLD MARKET

One of the major changes experienced by market-driven corporations has been a rethinking of the market in which each company operates.

That rethinking first focused on the product mix offered for sale; later it shifted to the geographic marketplace in which the products were offered. The growing trend toward this kind of rethinking has altered the marketplace so thoroughly that a short clarification of terms and ideas may be helpful:

- *Foreign trade.* A number of companies have always offered their products for sale in the export market—that market outside the company's home country. A number of companies have also purchased products through an import market—that is, from outside the home country. Because businesses and their governments viewed such transactions as uncommon and potentially harmful to domestic businesses, governments imposed tariffs and other restrictions to make such transactions difficult to perform. The result was that local national markets developed, protected from competition. Marketers could not easily do business under such conditions.

- *International trade.* As companies began to view sales across international borders as a part of regular business, they began pressuring their governments and those of other countries to ease cross-border restrictions. Over time, a number of cross-border agreements were worked out to ease the flow of business in and out of the country. *Bilateral tariffs* are international tariffs between two countries, granting particular products special standing at the borders of the participating countries; Canada and the United States have had a favored-nation bilateral tariff agreement on a number of products for many years. In such cases, it is not uncommon for products from the two countries to be used interchangeably. The auto industry, for instance, has benefitted from a tariff that permits automotive parts to be produced and purchased in Canada and the United States without being subject to restriction or duty. Such arrangements make marketing between such nations easier and thus more common.

- *Multilateral trade.* In recent years, the pressure from companies wishing to do business across political borders has increased significantly. The result has been a growing number of multilateral tariff agreements—agreements among several nations to treat their products as interchangeable. The largest such agreement is the European Economic Community (EEC) treaty and tariff agreement, which has resulted in a decreasing set of tariffs for nations within Western Europe and a common set of restrictive tariffs for other nations. While the EEC tariff treaty is not the first multilateral trading agreement, it is by far the largest and most comprehensive such arrangement and is causing review and adjustments of tariffs around the world.

The culmination of the EEC agreement has resulted in a flurry of activity on the North American continent. The United States has had limited multilateral tariffs with some Latin American nations for many years. Canada and the United States have recently eliminated virtually all restrictions of trade between them; at this writing, the United States, Canada, and Mexico are continuing negotiations aimed at creating a free trade zone among the three countries, which would allow marketers to plan strategy without reference to political borders while continuing to pay attention to differing cultures.

As companies do more international business, they and their home governments are realizing that all seem to prosper from such trade. As more countries lower their tariffs, they find that their own economies do not suffer despite some predictions to that effect. There is reason to believe that shifting and altering tariffs will continue to be an important issue for some time to come.

THE AGE OF THE MULTINATIONAL ORGANIZATION

The elimination of national tariffs and their replacement by multinational tariffs made it possible for more and more business to be done across national borders and around the world. This has changed the relationship of the marketplace, as well as of the competition. No company can assume that its own market is safe from competition, nor can it shrink from seeking success in other countries.

This change in attitude results in a basic restructuring of competition and corporate behavior, and thus in marketing strategy. Corporations are becoming multinational in their thinking and in their structure. Some companies have always operated internationally, but the changes taking place in the marketplace are making such positioning more desirable.

Some companies attempting to dominate markets in other countries join forces with their own competitors or with other multinationals in order to attempt to dominate second- or third-region markets. Several examples of corporate activity demonstrating the shift taking place in the multinational market illustrate this point:

- *U.S. makers invade the European sneaker market.* Nike and Reebok, which between them market more than 50 percent of the sneakers sold in the United States, are driving hard in the European market. They found an attractive opportunity when the two giant German sneaker manufacturers, Adidas and Puma, became complacent, having dominated the European market for many years. Nike took advantage of an additional opportunity by moving quickly to obtain endorsements from a number of East German star Olympic athletes, enabling it to compete with Adidas, which had signed most Western European athletes to endorsements. The German companies, both with new owners, are beginning to fight back.

- *Two giants combine for worldwide distribution.* Nestlé S.A. of Vevey, Switzerland, and the Coca-Cola Company of Atlanta, Georgia, formed a joint venture, Coca-Cola Nestlé Refreshments Company, in order to provide Nestlé products access to Coke's comprehensive 170-country distribution system. The result is effective access to a worldwide market, and thus marketing opportunities, for Nestlé products.

- *Once traditional European beer makers react to changing tastes.* With the elimination of tariff barriers across Western Europe, the nature of the beer market is changing. Assisting that change is the beginning of a shift in taste among Europeans as they become more weight- and calorie-conscious. Until recently, small brewers from each European country produced beer that was purchased by loyal local customers. During the later part of the 1980s, however, when European economic integration seemed likely, large European breweries began purchasing the local brewers; recently, U.S. brewers have joined in purchasing a number of local European breweries. Aided by changing customer values and a greater appreciation among Europeans of the American life style, together with their vast marketing experience, U.S. brewers hope to gain substantial market share in the upcoming donnybrook.

- *Japanese penetrate the American car market.* As more and more U.S. consumers have purchased imported Japanese cars, American automakers and politicians have placed pressure on the U.S. government to limit imports of the Japanese products. To get around that obstacle, Japanese marketers convinced manufacturers to construct auto production plants in the United States to build their cars. The unexpected result of this action has been to force the American Big Three auto companies finally to look seriously at their production and marketing techniques, something they have been avoiding doing for many years.

- *Sony Corp. takes the lead as an American entertainment giant.* Seeking to enhance its opportunity to market its stereos, TVs, cameras, tapes, discs, and other entertainment equipment and products, Sony has purchased Columbia Pictures, CBS Records, Columbia House records and tapes, and several supporting companies. Through this combination, Sony marketers will be able to provide videos, tapes, and discs of famous American artists and programs on formats produced by Sony. This will increase sales of both the "software" and the "hardware." It will also permit many tie-in promotional arrangements, which should prove beneficial to effective marketing of Sony products.

In this chapter, we have given the nonmarketer a sense of the dynamic changes occurring in business and how marketers are affected by them. These changes have, for instance, eliminated any serious discussion of a domestic market as such and substituted the world market, with submarket cultural targets, in its place.

PART TWO

Assessing the
Marketing Opportunity

CHAPTER 3

Market Intelligence as a Competitive Edge

Seeking a competitive edge is every manager's job. It can be sought through manufacturing, research and development, finance, distribution, sales, customer service, or any other functional area. Consider the definition of marketing presented in Chapter 1: a total system of interacting business activities designed to plan, price, promote, and distribute want-satisfying products and services to organizational and household users at a profit in a competitive environment. Involving managers in achieving a state of competitive readiness is consistent with our definition.

The business management team is the embodiment of the concept of interaction among managers. And the document that houses each manager's input and then outputs it in the form of competitive strategies is the *strategic marketing plan*. Nonmarketing managers can not only input valuable intelligence into the strategic marketing plan but can direct their own job functions.

Market intelligence (MI) is the gathering, processing, and interpreting of relevant information useful to management within categories related to environmental, industrial, customer, and competitor issues. These four categories help determine the strategic direction within the strategic marketing plan. In addition, there are numerous other questions to be considered in developing the planning guidelines that help shape objectives, determine strategies, and develop a business portfolio of markets and products.

Answering those planning questions, which are the subject of Chapters 6 and 7, requires data; those data that are processed and interpreted become market intelligence. Market intelligence equips nonmarketing managers with insights that add greater precision to decisions in some or all of the following categories:

- Identifying potential new market segments for growth and expansion, as Mitsubishi Electric did with its large-screen TVs
- Protecting a position against competitor inroads; for example, the fighting-back strategy of Motorola with its innovative new electronic products
- Analyzing the marketing mix and its components for possible modification; for example, improved product quality, add-on services, just-in-time (JIT) delivery, and additional warranties, all used by Black & Decker to strengthen its market position
- Providing feedback on product usage, performance, and reliability to product developers for generating product life-cycle extension strategies; used by Procter & Gamble (P&G) to get closer to its customers
- Evaluating product differentiation strategies to avoid facing an undifferentiated commodity situation (Black & Decker)
- Expanding product usage through new applications (Mitsubishi)
- Monitoring on a competitor-by-competitor basis threats to market segments and to total market share and then recommending strategies to protect market share (P&G)
- Evaluating options such as focusing on a specific market niche, extending the market, locating export opportunities, or forming joint ventures with manufacturers, distributors, or suppliers (Motorola)
- Identifying poorly served customer segments as an idea generator for new-product development (Mitsubishi)

To help you understand how you can participate in the MI process, we next examine types of MI, sources of MI, and methods of collecting MI.

TYPES OF MARKET INTELLIGENCE

MI encompasses the four broad classifications listed earlier: environmental, industrial, customer, and competitor issues. Understanding the makeup of each permits you to make meaningful contributions to these categories.

Environmental Issues

Environmental issues include these factors:

- *Demographics.* Segments or clusters of customers are classified by sex, age, family life cycle, race/ethnicity, education, income, occupation, family size, religion, and home ownership. Organizations such as P&G, Sears, Roebuck, and McDonald's use this information to make product development, pricing, and merchandising decisions.

- *Economics.* Economic factors include global, national, and regional income levels of groups; employment/unemployment rates by geographic segment; effects of rate of saving and debt burden by buying groups; and patterns of spending for the immediate future and the long term. Managers of consumer, service, and industrial organizations use the data to control resources, determine inventory levels, and identify products to suit specific economic conditions.

- *Natural resources.* Natural resources refer to the availability of specific resources such as platinum, gold, zinc, and lead, as well as energy resources such as oil and coal. This information is important to product developers and those involved in manufacturing and R&D, who may need to find alternative sources of reliable energy. The information also is helpful in determining favorable geographic locations for plants that need to be in proximity to suppliers. It is also useful intelligence for those organizations that are facing major capital expenditures and are concerned about the availability of natural resources.

- *Technology.* This area focuses on levels of expenditures in technology—the degree of sophistication compared to the standards of the industry or product category. The future belongs to those organizations that can use technology to satisfy the increasingly complex demands of markets and customers. Merck, AT&T, Dow Chemical, Kodak, IBM, and Eli Lilly all spend at above-average rates for research. To bolster its R&D capability, Inland Steel formed a joint venture with Nippon Steel, thereby becoming one of the most technologically advanced U.S. steelmakers.

- *Legislation.* This area considers the impact of changing political, legal, and regulatory issues at the federal, state, and local levels. The market intelligence pertains to major laws protecting competition, consumers, and the larger interests of society and the environment. For all companies, a continuous flow of information is required to identify problems and opportunities related to minority rights, senior citizen rights, women's rights, and consumer rights.

■ *Sociocultural values.* This area considers both the beliefs and values of a society's cultures and subcultures. Particular cultural groupings have similar beliefs and values, which tend to differ from those of other cultural groupings, on topics such as work, marriage, and family. MI studies the effect of values and beliefs on the types of products and services purchased and how media and messages can influence various groups. Many companies today go beyond demographic breakdowns and observe life styles for clues to new designs, purchase behavior, and trends. Nissan Motor Company, for example, employs anthropologists to probe into what makes people buy cars and then translates that research into subtle new features that give products a distinctive advantage.

Industrial Issues

Gathering industry market intelligence is complex. The topic covers a diverse range of factors, depending on where a company operates within an industry (manufacturer, service provider, supplier, or retailer). However, common factors guide what intelligence should be gathered and evaluated for its strategic value.

Factors worth knowing about include the current demand for a product, the product's potential, emerging technologies, changing customer profiles, frequency of new product entries, and cost structures. Overall, however, to provide structure to the major categories where industry market intelligence is valuable, researchers use the following breakdown:

■ *Suppliers.* This topic covers the availability of supplies and suppliers and the power exerted by suppliers over prices and the availability of materials. Such intelligence has strategy implications in evaluating joint ventures and foreign alliances. Motorola saw the wisdom of forming joint ventures with Toyota and IBM; in part, the agreement ensured the availability of microchips and technology.

■ *Existing competitors.* This intelligence serves to interpret the strategies of competitors—their aggressiveness in boosting market share, differentiating products to avoid a commodity situation, developing into a low-cost producer, or using price wars to reduce the number of competitors. Understanding competitors' strategies is the foundation upon which counterstrategies are shaped. Black & Decker exerted a great deal of effort in rebuilding its market position in power tools by understanding the strategies of its competitors, Makita and Skil. Since this is the most critical area of market intelligence, it is discussed in more depth later in this chapter.

- *Emerging competitors.* This area of intelligence concentrates on those companies that at first had a minor presence in a market segment and later became a threat after an infusion of cash and technology gained through acquisition of or joint venture with another organization. Other organizations, broadening their strategic direction, may launch into a market in which they had no prior penetration. Mitsubishi, for example, was once a presence only in heavy industry but has since moved into the consumer electronics market with its large-screen TVs.

- *Alternative product offerings.* This form of intelligence alerts marketing and nonmarketing managers to a competitor's use of substitute products and materials. Such information serves as an early warning system, permitting time for evaluating alternative actions to solve an impending competitive problem or to develop an opportunity. The auto industry provides a familiar example of how aluminum replaced steel in many applications and how plastics increasingly provide an alternative to aluminum.

Customer Issues

The focal point of all the market intelligence discussed so far is the customer. To produce want-satisfying products and services, managers must know what customers want, where customers can find what they want, and how to convince customers that one company is able to meet their needs better than a competitor.

Customers are classified at all stages of the buying cycle. The categories include end-use consumers and industrial and commercial buyers, as well as intermediaries such as distributors, wholesalers, and retailers. Each stage represents a force within an industry that warrants market intelligence. Answering the following questions provides the base upon which information is assembled:

- Is there sufficient product differentiation, or can customers simply switch from one supplier (domestic or foreign) to another?

- Do customers tend to dictate buying terms because of large-volume purchases?
- Are changes in customers' demographics or buying patterns emerging that signal problems in maintaining your market position? Do emerging trends suggest opportunities in new market segments?
- Are customers knowledgeable about costs of raw materials and manufacturing, and do they use such information as bargaining power?

Competitor Issues

We have discussed this subject briefly earlier in this chapter (under industrial MI), but the subject is sufficiently important to be singled out for fuller discussion here. Through a comprehensive analysis of competitors' intentions, managers can position their product, leverage their distribution strength, focus their salesforce, determine their advertising theme, and calculate their prices.

Knowing competitors' strategies through a strength-and-weakness analysis, which highlights strategies for positioning your resources to attack your competitors' areas of weakness, prevents direct conflict in the marketplace, which tends to consume resources. It's important to gather competitor intelligence with purpose and to distinguish between usable information and nice-to-know information. You can systematize the intelligence-gathering process by using the following structured list of questions. (Sources of intelligence will be identified later in this chapter.)

Market

- In what size market does each competitor operate?
- How do competitors usually enter a market?
- Is there a market leader among competitors? Who are the followers?
- How much commitment do competitors give to a specific market in terms of priorities and resources?
- How flexible are competitors in changing strategies for different market situations?
- How have competitors responded to diversification opportunities?

Product

- How efficient are competitors in monitoring customer perceptions and identifying customer niches?
- How efficient are competitors in extending the life cycle of their products?
- To what extent do competitors attempt to gain a larger market share by introducing new products?
- How do competitors compare in width and depth of product lines?
- How much manufacturing and design flexibility do competitors display?
- What has been the pattern of competitors in relation to new-product development?
- How flexible have competitors been in monitoring their product lines for expansion or reduction?

Price

- What has been the pattern of competitors in pricing new products?
- What has been the pattern of competitors in pricing established products?

Promotion

- To what extent do competitors use advertising to support the selling activity, rather than promote the total company?
- What are the profiles of competitors' sales forces?
- How well do competitors integrate sales promotion into their advertising and salesforce strategies?

Distribution

- What distribution strategies do competitors use in reaching markets?
- Are competitors employing new strategies that might alter their distribution patterns?
- Are competitors adding channels that complement or compete against existing ones to reach new markets?

Answering all or most of these questions puts you and your group in a better competitive position to be proactive against competition and changing market conditions and leaves you in a better position to contribute to business plans and contingency plans.

SOURCES OF MARKET INTELLIGENCE

Every market-driven company uses a large quantity of market intelligence: facts about the marketing mix (product, price, promotion, and distribution); data about the company's assets, liabilities, and long-term plans; information about competing companies and their products; statistics about the market and the general economy; and trends in customer habits, attitudes, and behavior.

An important part of collecting data lies in knowing the sources of market intelligence. Data are derived from either primary or secondary sources. *Primary data* are original information collected for a particular project. *Secondary data* are information collected by someone else for another purpose but that may be applicable to the company's problem or opportunity. These terms refer not to the value or usefulness of the data but to their source.

Primary and secondary data can be either internal or external. *Internal data* are collected from within the company itself. *External data* are collected from sources outside the company. Most market intelligence activities require both types of data; each type has its own characteristics, advantages, and disadvantages.

PRIMARY DATA

Primary data have two important advantages over secondary data: (1) the precise facts needed for a specific decision can be obtained, and (2) collections of data not available from any other source can be built up. For instance, the manager of a women's clothing shop in a suburban shopping mall might find it difficult to base her choice of inventory on secondary data; what the average customer in the average store wants in skirt lengths may not match the taste of her own select group of customers. Instead of relying on secondary data, the manager would be in a much better position if she were to collect primary data, probably by conducting a survey of her customers. She would then be in a better position to know what kind of stock her customers would buy.

The major disadvantage of primary data collection is that it usually involves a considerable investment of time, money, personnel, and facilities. Whether the results are worth that investment is an important decision. Consider the clothing shop owner. She may have to hire a trained interviewer to question everyone who comes into the store during a two-week period. Such a project involves not only the cost of the interviewer and of tabulating and analyzing the data collected but the inevitable slowdown of business as customers sit down and chat instead of concentrating on making purchases.

As long as the data collected and the decisions involved concern the major profit-producing segment of the business (the inventory of clothing), it is probably a worthwhile investment. On the other hand, it would be a waste of money and time to make a survey of what customers think about minor accessories, which represent a very small portion of the shop's inventory.

SECONDARY DATA

A baby food company executive studying the new birthrate statistics released regularly by the Bureau of the Census is using secondary data. The information is collected by the Census Bureau for the federal government; its usefulness and interest to a manufacturer is secondary to the original reason for collecting it. But manufacturers need this information; nowhere else could they obtain such detailed figures about their particular group of customers, unless, of course, they were to set up their own private census units, requiring an investment of time and money that would be unrealistic.

Secondary information has three general advantages over primary information: (1) it is easier to obtain, (2) it is less expensive to obtain, and (3) some facts are available only in the form of secondary data (for even if a manufacturer did set up his own private census, he would have no right to demand that people answer his questions, a right that the federal government does have).

The major disadvantage of secondary data is that the user has no control over the original collection of the data and does not know how accurately, scientifically, or honestly the data were gathered. Some organizations that collect and distribute data do so for a promotional purpose or for a motive that may not be obvious, such as supplying potential advertisers with favorable statistics on the readership of a magazine. This is not to imply that the average organization deliberately distorts or changes figures but to point out that it simply organizes and displays information in its own best interest; different infer-ences can be drawn from a single set of figures, depending on how the figures are listed and analyzed.

Most sources of basic secondary data, however, are honest and unbiased. The gatherers are willing to explain how they collected the data, what sources and methods they used, and how they recorded figures and analyzed them. With this information, managers can then decide whether or not the data are valuable for their purpose.

Sources of Secondary Data

A researcher usually begins the search for market intelligence by con-sidering whatever data are available within the company itself. Inter-nal data tend to be inexpensive and easy to locate, and the facts have the obvious advantage of already being geared to the company itself. Next, the manager examines various sources of external data. Obtain-ing external data from secondary sources is usually—but not neces-sarily—more expensive than using internal sources. External data can be more time-consuming to locate, and unless a special firm is hired to collect specific data, what is collected often contains considerable needless material. That means the manager has to spend time sifting through a great many facts and figures before finding the ones that will be useful. Nevertheless, compared with developing primary data, using secondary data is still the cheapest and quickest way, and some-times the only way, to obtain the necessary information.

Internal Sources of Secondary Data. Ideally, marketing and non-marketing managers are working toward a common goal: sustaining the long-term economic health of their markets and maintaining their company's profitable position in those markets. Any information gen-erated within a company should be freely available to and exchanged with any unit or department within the organization, regardless of its size. Unfortunately, the ideal is seldom realized. In some large com-panies, departments tend to be parochial about their own collections of data, preferring to retain them for their own use.

In large and small companies alike, establishing multifunctional planning teams helps alleviate some communications problems by keeping managers involved in tracking data, particularly if there is no central data-collection system. Under this approach, managers from several different areas of a company or division are assigned the re-sponsibility for data identification, collection, collation, and review. By meeting regularly, such teams provide an interchange of ideas, a broad perspective on issues, and involvement from many sources.

Multifunctional planning teams are an ideal way for nonmarketers to become involved in marketing decisions and to obtain a better understanding of marketing issues and problems.

The initial source of internal data is the accounting department, whether it consists of a large staff and a building full of records or a ledger and a file drawer. The next stop is the sales department. The third possibility is to check the files of whatever divisions or departments do any work related to a particular marketing problem or opportunity. The major sources of readily available data within a company are:

- Financial statements, including the balance sheet and the profit-and-loss statement
- Sales records for customer, product line, product, size of order, frequency of purchase
- The accounts-receivable ledger or customer ledger
- The file of customer orders
- Sales compensation records, including salaries and commissions
- Sales expense reports, including expenses for travel, hotel, meals, and entertainment
- Sales reports (daily, weekly, and summary)

The information in these standard accounting and marketing records can be analyzed according to product, customer, geographic area, or whatever topic the manager has in mind. For instance, facts about the profitability of a particular product can be found in just about every one of these records. The profit-and-loss statement shows the ratio of profits made by this product to those made by all products combined. The file of customer orders might indicate whether supply of the product is keeping up with customer demand. Sales compensation records indicate whether the salespeople handling the product are having problems moving it, while expense records show how much selling investment it takes to sell the product. The sales records themselves show where the product is within its probable life cycle.

In addition to the information provided by the basic records, the company has price lists, customer correspondence, and service records. Many companies have built up collections of data used in other areas of planning that might be useful to the manager in any area of market research. A researcher in a large company can spend a long time exploring company sources of information before running out of material. Even in small companies, normal records contain far more information than many managers realize.

Still other sources of internal information include engineers, scientists, and other technical people who have access to data—and the expertise to interpret the implications of the data—from professional societies, trade publications, technical consultants, and academic institutions.

Additional sources that are sometimes overlooked are purchasing agents, who can provide information on sources of supply and new materials being offered, and human resources managers, who can provide useful information on their contacts with individuals from competing companies.

External Sources of Secondary Data. A manager can learn much from the company's own files, but external sources are more likely to indicate trends in the marketplace, in customer preference, and in competition. Investigating these sources can involve considerable time if a researcher must hunt through library shelves seeking the information needed to piece together a collection of facts, or it can be as simple as writing to an organization and requesting a specific list, chart, or brochure. Useful outside sources of secondary information include libraries, advertising agencies and media, market research agencies, trade associations, universities and foundations, the government, and electronic data base sources.

Libraries. A tremendous amount of secondary data in the literature is carried by libraries of all kinds, both public and private. Managers of smaller companies will find that the local public library has a surprising amount of information on its reference shelves; those in organizations may want to explore the collections of libraries in universities, institutions, and even other large companies in the field.

Public libraries are open to all; university, institution, and company libraries are usually open to anyone who can give a logical reason for wanting to examine their material. Librarians are usually available to give some help in locating information, but outside users have to do much of the work themselves.

Source guides to help track down specific books and magazines for pertinent data include:

- *The library's listings catalog.* Lists all the books and periodicals contained in the library by subject, title, and author. These listings are now typically computerized. Even local library catalogs frequently provide listings on the holdings of other libraries within a given regional area.

- *Business Periodicals Index.* A cumulative listing of all articles appearing in the business press, by subject.
- *Monthly Catalog of U.S. Government Publications.* A listing of all publications put out by the federal government during the preceding month, arranged alphabetically by name of the issuing bureau.
- *Marketing Information Guide.* A summary, issued monthly by the U.S. Department of Commerce, of the major marketing and distribution books, reports, and articles.
- *New York Times Index.* Synopses of articles in that newspaper, with reference to date and page/section location.
- *Wall Street Journal Index.* Either the headline or a synopsis of each of that newspaper's articles.

A number of books that contain information about where to find what facts are published and updated regularly. Many volumes of condensed and summary statistics are published regularly in pamphlet or book form, primarily by the federal government. Although librarians seldom have the time to locate the exact information a manager needs, they are always willing to suggest the books that provide the right material.

Advertising Agencies and Media. Most advertising agencies and the media they serve (newspapers, magazines, television and radio stations, and networks) have set up their own research departments to serve managers interested in using advertising in the media. Most of their research effort concentrates on the customers reached in the particular medium and the effectiveness of certain types of advertising.

Agency research tends to be quite specialized; agencies sometimes undertake a special project for a company. Media research is often more promotional than professional, its goal being to promote a particular medium as the right place for the marketing campaign. Although reputable research departments do not distort the results of their research, it is wise to remember that the facts most readily available from such sources are those that encourage advertising in the media. However, this type of research can produce many interesting and useful facts about a given industry.

The results of media research are usually handed out freely, often published as giveaway information by the medium itself. Advertising agencies absorb some of the costs of obtaining data in their regular commissions on the sale of advertising, reserving a fee for any special research work they agree to perform.

Market Research Agencies. Market research has become such an important activity in its own right that a number of companies have been set up just to specialize in it. Market research work is done by two types of companies: consulting firms and syndicated data firms. They and any other companies that engage in market research make use of market research service firms.

Consulting firms in the market research field specialize in solving specific marketing problems brought to them by clients. They work for a client as independent contractors who do a specified job for a specified fee. Most consulting firms employ relatively small staffs of trained specialists and often handle work only within a specific industry or field. Anyone knowledgeable in a particular industry can recommend reputable consulting market research firms in that industry; local banks and business bureaus can also suggest names of local firms.

Syndicated data firms specialize in collecting certain types of information and then selling the information on a subscription basis. Thus, a syndicated data firm does research for others in a general way, but it does not undertake to study a specific problem for a specific company. Such a firm usually concentrates on a particular industry or a particular kind of information. Typical specialties include surveys of brand recognition, public opinion, fashion trends, advertising volume, and traffic counts. Among the larger and better known syndicated data firms are A. C. Nielsen, Market Research Corporation of America, Daniel Starch and Staff, Gallup and Robinson, the F. W. Dodge Corporation, and R. L. Polk Company.

Market research service companies neither collect data nor conduct any facet of basic research, yet they provide a service for those who do. Most firms specialize in one form of service, such as providing trained interviewers, tabulating personnel and equipment, and creating printed and bound research reports. *FINDEX, the Directory of Market Research Reports, Studies and Surveys* is an excellent source of published marketing research organization information.

Trade Associations. Every trade association gradually builds up a fund of information about the industry or field it serves. Seldom does a trade association undertake research for an individual member. Most of the data that a trade association does collect are available to member companies.

Most trade associations collect periodic reports on members' operating figures. Although the figures each company supplies are usually kept confidential, they are used to work out statistical tables that show the typical, average, or median figures reported. These statistics are useful in gauging the operating trends among members; if the association is important enough in its industry or field, the figures obtained reflect the industry or field as a whole.

The advantage of trade association figures is that they tend to be the only unbiased figures available for the industry as a whole. Yet, because such organizations are not primarily set up as research organizations, the data are neither collected nor analyzed in the most scientific way. Furthermore, the average figures may be based on a very small sampling of the industry.

Universities and Foundations. Most state universities and many private universities now have business research bureaus or departments that do basic work in collecting useful business information. These bureaus or departments seldom undertake a project for a specific company unless that project is one whose results will benefit the industry or the business world as a whole. Here, the subject of the research is determined by the university, the work is handled by the university, and the results are then made available in published form to anyone who is interested.

In addition to groups within the universities, there are also a number of research organizations affiliated with universities that conduct basic marketing research. The better known of these are the Stanford Research Institute, the National Opinion Research Center of the University of Chicago, and the Survey Research Center of the University of Michigan. Again, results usually appear in published form, either as an article or a book.

Foundations also do considerable research. Those foundations most likely to be involved in marketing research and thus most likely to have marketing data available include the Brookings Institution, the National Industrial Conference Board, the National Bureau for Economic Research, and the Twentieth Century Fund.

Most of the publications put out by universities and foundations alike are reviewed or listed in one of the guides discussed in the section on libraries. In fact, the local public library is one of the best places for the novice to begin a secondary data collection, for it usually houses a fairly wide selection of material from all kinds of sources.

Federal Government. The largest single source of secondary marketing data is the federal government. Surveys made by the Bureau of the Census provide the foundation for the entire structure of marketing knowledge in the United States; these surveys are supplemented by research done by other bureaus within the federal government, such as the Bureau of Labor Statistics, the Federal Power Commission, and the Bureau of Agricultural Economics.

In addition to simply collecting data, some federal agencies do other types of research as well. For instance, what regulations or standards are needed in a particular industry or field? The by-product of the research may be an interesting collection of new data. The Federal Trade Commission, the Food and Drug Administration, and the Federal Communications Commission have carried out elaborate research whose results are available to anyone.

The vast collections of data produced by the federal government are available in printed form for remarkably low prices. The local library can provide information about what is available, but those who live in areas that have a regional office of the Department of Commerce, which is the parent of the Bureau of the Census, should investigate the services of that office. Those offices with well-trained staffs and good supplies of material can produce an array of data in a remarkably short time.

State and Local Government. Agencies of the state and local government abound with information that may prove helpful. Such data vary both in quality and quantity by state and local governing agency. Where it is available and accurate, it is particularly useful because it is more local in nature than data compiled by the federal government. The more local or regional the data, the more likely they are to reflect important trends in the area of most interest to a regional company.

At the state level, valuable data can be obtained from the license bureaus, ranging from automobile to liquor authority boards. Typical data include construction figures, state income and property tax figures, population and industry-reported figures, and state employee salary figures, to mention but a few. Each state issues an almanac or state-of-the-state message handbook, which contains large amounts of current or budgeted data. The larger industrial states, such as New York, California, and Illinois, provide substantial amounts of carefully and thoroughly collected information. Local governments are a good source of information on home starts, utility connections, tax-rate data on homes and businesses, real estate transactions, registration fees for business operations, and local tax assessments.

Electronic Data Base Sources. The use of computers has revolutionized the intelligence-gathering activity. Nonmarketing managers should know what is available and what the huge expansion of data means to corporate success.

The growth of on-line data bases in the United States, and to a lesser degree in other countries, is making information available on a scale hardly imagined a little over a decade ago. For example, 400 data bases existed in 1980; 4,465 were available by 1990. And the number of data base producers has expanded from 221 to 1,950 during the same period, according to the *Directory of Online Databases*, published by Elsevier.

Gale Research's *Computer Readable Data Bases* directory reports that almost 70 percent of the on-line data bases are located in the United States. Increasingly, however, new data bases are proliferating in other parts of the world. For example, the Japan Center for Information and Cultural Affairs translates Japanese government documents, statistics on Japan, and information on trade groups in that country. In addition, the European Community has created a data base to provide researchers with up-to-date information on European trends and issues. A Luxembourg-based data base known as The Echo includes competitive and financial information.

While the need for market intelligence is vital to corporate success, the actual use of the vast amount of data in an organized fashion has been spotty. Only a few organizations stand out as applying computer technology to its fullest.

Corning Glass, Digital Equipment, and AT&T are models of companies immersed in computer networks for gathering market intelligence. Users of Corning's Global Business Information Exchange Network, for example, inform the system of topics that interest them. The system then automatically identifies articles and places them in the users' electronic mail box. Digital Equipment's system, which includes Corning's features, focuses on both strategic and tactical needs. The system contains product descriptions and announcements; internal and external competitive analyses; company strategies, policies, and overviews; market analyses; and a direct feed from an external news wire.

AT&T maintains a sophisticated system with features similar to those of Corning and Digital Equipment. One impressive addition to the system is the widespread availability of market intelligence, which serves over 1,000 users at 257 locations. Its user-friendly features also permit computer novices to access the information, thereby permitting all levels of functional managers to enhance their work through a market-directed flow of data. Such widespread availability of information permits further interpretation and increases the level of insight that can be applied to the planning process.

Of the thousands of data bases, some of the more popular ones are the New York Times Information Bank and the Dow-Jones News Retrieval Databases, both of which cover general and business news. Other data bases provide information on specific subjects or industries, such as electronics or oil. The field is exploding so rapidly that directories are needed to keep up to date on the latest data bases. Such directories, published by Gale Research Company, R. R. Bowker Company, and Information Industry Association, are obtainable from those companies and are available at many libraries.

METHODS OF COLLECTING PRIMARY DATA

Primary data are original information collected for a specific purpose. The manager may handle the research job internally or may hire a research firm to do the work. Regardless of who does the work, the project is tailored to the specific data requirements of the strategic marketing plan.

Three basic methods are used to collect primary data: the survey method, the observation method, and the experimentation method. Each has its own advantages and disadvantages. The one to use depends on such factors as the kind of information needed, the accuracy and objectivity required, and the time, money, personnel, and facilities available.

The Survey Method

The process of contacting people for specific kinds of information is the survey method of collecting data. The contact is usually made in person, over the telephone, and/or through the mail; the people contacted may be everyone in a particular group, such as all the members of a trade association, or a sampling of a group, such as every twentieth name in the local telephone directory; the kinds of information sought may be hard facts or opinions.

The survey is the most widely used method of collecting primary data. The value of the data depends on how the survey is organized and carried out; every aspect of a survey must be carefully planned and executed if the results are to be worth the time and money spent.

Although surveys can be done by the smallest companies, they are particularly popular with some of the largest organizations. A specialty shop owner may stand in the aisle of his store several hours a day for two or three days, asking customers five or six questions and then mentally analyzing their answers to help pinpoint any changes in what his customers want. A large store can collect this same kind of information by sending a questionnaire to each of its charge account customers. (Electronic means of surveying are discussed later in this chapter.)

A survey can cost very little, or it can run into a considerable expenditure. A personal interview, for instance, can cost anywhere from around $25 to $500 for each person interviewed, depending on the qualifications of the interviewer, the travel costs involved, the type of person being interviewed, and the length of the interview.

Forms to Use. The most commonly used survey forms are the interview and the questionnaire. The *interview* is a survey conducted by one person with either one other person or a small group of persons, face-to-face or over the telephone. The *questionnaire* is a printed survey mailed or handed to an individual; sometimes questionnaires are printed in a newspaper or magazine with the suggestion that readers answer the questions and mail in the form.

The interview form of survey has the advantage of flexibility. The interviewer can adapt or change the questions according to the response of the person being interviewed. A trained interviewer can also ask for, and usually get, more kinds of information than can be requested on a questionnaire, because many people will answer some questions orally that they will not answer on paper. Finally, a skilled interviewer can often sense attitudes and opinions of the person being interviewed, even when these are not put directly into words.

A *focus group* is a special type of interview. A focus group consists of a small number of people with similar characteristics or interests. They may be mothers with small children, women interested in clothing or cosmetics, or people interested in electronic equipment. The interviewer in a focus group is interested in learning not only about reactions of each individual but also in the dialog that develops concerning the product, as the participants carry on a back-and-forth discussion. The approach is particularly useful in the consumer products market.

The unstructured nature of many interviews can become a disadvantage if the interviewer isn't thoroughly trained. If an interviewer misinterprets answers or makes mistakes in recording information, those mistakes will lead to a bias in the final data. There is more chance for human error in the interview than there is in the questionnaire method.

Telephone surveys are becoming increasingly popular. Such surveys are usually the least expensive of the interview techniques, and they have become increasingly easy to use because of the sophisticated services now offered by telephone companies. However, lengthy questioning usually cannot be handled over the telephone, and there are many kinds of information—especially that dealing with income and material wealth—that people may be willing to discuss in person but that they would be unwilling to discuss with an anonymous telephone voice for fear of robberies or burglaries.

Questionnaires have some important advantages. By using the mail, researchers can survey a broad range of people in many geographic areas at the same time. In addition, people who fill in questionnaires usually take the time to consider their answers carefully, and they seldom worry about wording their answers to impress anyone. Questionnaires are an excellent technique, provided that enough people reply to make their answers representative of the group as a whole. Many companies consider themselves lucky to get a 10 percent rate of response; others, using a variety of incentives from inserting a dollar bill with the questionnaire to awarding a prize, may boost the rate of response to 30 percent or more. In addition to the difficulty of getting enough people to answer, researchers face the problems of compiling or finding good mailing lists, setting up good questionnaires, and paying the steadily increasing postage rates.

Whom to Survey. Choosing the survey target can either be a very simple job or a very complex one. The choice makes or breaks the validity of the data obtained. If everyone in a group is surveyed, as in the case of the members of the trade association or the charge account customers of the store, there is no problem. If a sample has to be picked, the task becomes more difficult.

A sample is a limited selection of persons chosen because they are representative of a larger group. Various techniques are used by researchers in choosing samples. One of the most common is random sampling, in which each member of the total group has an equal chance of being included. Choosing names by chance from the local telephone directory is an example of random sampling. Nonprobability or weighted sampling is a method of selection that deliberately includes a particular proportion of people with specified characteristics. A very simplified example might be that of a manufacturer with fifty wholesaler customers and one hundred retailer customers; the manufacturer in this case might weight the sample to contain two retailers for each wholesaler surveyed.

Some companies prepare their own samples; others depend on professional list-compiling companies. Professionally compiled lists are almost always used for mailed questionnaires or mailed advertising rather than for interviewing purposes. List companies can put together practically any kind of list a company can imagine. The price for using a tailored list (for lists are usually rented rather than sold) depends on how specialized the list is. For instance, a list of people who have bought houses within a particular area within the past two years is relatively easy to compile and therefore relatively inexpensive to rent. But if that list were pruned to contain only the names of those with net incomes above a specified level and who purchased that house as a second home or a summer home, the list would cost more to rent, having cost more to compile—but it would be more valuable to the user because it would have fewer unwanted names in it.

Facts vs. Opinions. A survey may seek data in the form of either hard facts or opinions and attitudes. Facts are much easier to collect, but opinions and attitudes can be useful if they are collected carefully and acted upon early enough. For instance, facts about what customers in a particular market are buying today are useful for immediate and current production planning, but opinions about what customers will buy tomorrow, if valid, can help managers prioritize their future product development schedules.

The questions asked in an interview or on a questionnaire must be carefully prepared. They must be clearly stated and easily understood, yet not appear to pry or demand. Questions must be easy to answer and interesting enough so that the person being surveyed wants to answer them. They must be in logical sequence, so that one question leads naturally into the next, and designed so that one question does not influence the answer to the next. Most important, the questions must be phrased in such a manner as to obtain the kind of data the marketer is interested in without encouraging bias in the survey answers.

The flexibility of the interview allows the interviewer to explain or rephrase a question if the person being interviewed seems puzzled by it, as long as the interviewer doesn't bias the question in rephrasing it. It is also possible to learn much more about opinions and attitudes in an interview, since people respond more freely and at greater length to another person than they do when writing questions on paper.

The face-to-face interview is the best technique for drawing opinions and ideas from the person being interviewed; often such an interviewer is given considerable leeway in choosing the best way to present the questions. In contrast, the interviewer is more likely to stick to a set list of questions in a telephone interview in order to complete the interview within a specified amount of time.

A questionnaire must be completely self-explanatory. It must give instructions, encourage participation, and be easy to understand and fill in. Although opinions can be asked for on questionnaires, this form of inquiry is most useful when there is a need to collect hard facts. The federal census form distributed every ten years throughout the United States and wherever U.S. citizens are living is a good example of a hard-facts form. Age, income level, occupational category—such questions leave little room for confusion.

The Observation Method

What people say they do and what they actually do can be quite different. For this reason, and because it is the easiest and most accurate way to collect some types of data, the observation method, which involves observing and recording actions that actually take place, is widely used for some types of research.

The main advantage of the observation method is that it records actions. What people do is recorded as it is being done, not as people remember doing it. What happens is recorded as it happens, not as it is remembered or judged to have happened. For instance, a person might estimate that she turns on her television set an average of three nights a week for a period of two to three hours each night. Observation might show that she actually turns her television set on an average of four nights a week, one night playing it for about four hours and the other nights playing it for an average of about an hour a night.

The observation method also eliminates possible weighting of the data, whether conscious or unconscious, resulting from interviewer prejudice or bias. For instance, an interviewer might find some questions dull or confusing and consequently collect less data on those points during the survey. Or an interviewer might take an instinctive liking to a person being interviewed and give that person's answers more weight than they deserve.

The observation method has two disadvantages, however. It can be relatively costly, as it is likely to tie up trained people and expensive equipment for long periods of time, much of which is spent waiting for something to happen rather than recording actions. In addition, opinions and attitudes, so important in marketing, cannot be recorded, since they are states of mind, not actions. Two basic forms of the observation method are frequently used in market research—the personal and the mechanical/electronic method.

Personal Observation. Personal observation is particularly useful in various facets of retailing. A store often uses "shoppers," trained observers who shop different departments of the store and observe and record the behavior and actions of salespeople. A retailer considering opening a shop in a shopping center might copy down the license plate numbers of cars parking at the center during one week to determine the area from which the center is drawing its customers; a department manager might station a trained observer near an unusual display to observe and record the reactions of people who stop to examine the display. In each case, the technique records hard facts in the form of actions, resulting in a collection of data that probably could not be gathered in any other way.

Mechanical/Electronic Observation. Mechanical/electronic observation involves the use of recording equipment to observe and record data, in the form of impulses, photographs, or counts. The cord stretched across the highway that feeds an impulse into a recording unit every time a car passes over the cord provides an excellent, unbiased record of the number of automobiles using a specific route during a specific time period. The audimeter, used by various market research firms, records the exact time a television set is turned on and off as well as what stations it is tuned to.

In many stores, cameras and remote television sets are used to analyze the buying patterns of customers and monitor the flow of traffic in the various departments. Using such devices has the added advantage of enabling the store owners to guard stockroom areas and merchandise displays to prevent theft. Banks, too, use cameras to record all action that takes place at each cashier's window, creating a photographic record of any attempted holdup.

Related to observation is the increasing use of electronic scanning, particularly at the retail supermarket and department store levels. In addition to observing buying behavior in the aisle, these stores have checkout counters record the actual purchases through the use of over one million Universal Product Codes—the small panels of thin and thick lines that are affixed to virtually every product and that are read by the scanners. The detailed information, which can be communicated electronically through various EDI (electronic data interchange) systems to a manufacturer or supplier for automatic reordering, is further analyzed to target promotional campaigns to specific groups of buyers, to provide input for adding or deleting items from the product line, and to permit greater precision in formulating competitive strategies.

Companies such as A. C. Nielsen and a division of Citicorp collect market intelligence, then package the data to whatever specifications the customer wants and sell to corporate subscribers such as General Foods, Coca-Cola, Ralston Purina, and Clairol. Each subscriber is provided with data on its own company's products and on competing brands as well. The result is more accurate and timely market intelligence.

The Experimentation Method

Experimentation changes one or more factors to show the effect of that change under controlled conditions. Managers probably become involved in more experiments than they realize. Some of these are laboratory experiments, in which product production methods or product qualities are measured and tested. But the laboratory can also be the marketplace, where primary data can be collected by experimentation.

The setup for an experiment requires an experimental group and a control group. A change is introduced in the experimental group but not in the control group. After a period of time, both groups are examined to see whether the change has caused any variation between the experimental group and the control group and, if so, what that variation is.

Application in Marketing. Aside from the use of experiments as a method of collecting technical data about a product, the major use of the experimental method in marketing is to test variations in product, price, promotion, or distribution under actual market conditions. Experimentation is an important step in the introduction of a new product, as well as in helping to determine what changes are needed in an established product to keep it profitable.

For instance, suppose a company decides to strengthen its marketing mix by changing the packaging of one line of products. One, perhaps two, new types of packaging are developed and produced in a limited quantity. Three market areas, which are as similar as possible in all major respects, are chosen. The two new packaging designs are introduced in two of the areas, one in each area, and the third area is designated as the control area. After a set period of time, the company examines both the sales records produced by all three areas plus the customer comments that have been collected by salespeople. The resulting data might well show that one new packaging idea produces considerably more customer interest than either the other new design or the old design.

Sometimes an experiment has unusual results. The following is a simplified and edited version of what an experiment taught one manager. When the manager, who ran a men's shop with heavy emphasis on high-priced merchandise, decided to clear some excess inventory of summer shirts off the shelves, he marked some of them down 30 percent and some of them down 60 percent. His reasoning was that the few marked down 60 percent would be particularly attractive price leaders that would bring customers flocking to the store. When the sale was completed, he found he had sold most of those shirts that had been marked down 30 percent, yet he still had an excess of shirts marked down 60 percent. The data, when supplemented by a quick survey of the salespeople and a few customers, showed that the customers didn't trust too low a price, fearing that the product was inferior.

The Pros and Cons of Experimentation. The major advantage of experimentation lies in its realism. It is the only one of the three methods of collecting primary data that can be used to test a factor under actual or simulated market conditions. However, it often takes a long time for sufficient data to be collected to provide usable results, and it is often very hard to control adequately the conditions of an experiment adequately enough to yield valid results. While experimentation is a vital method for getting the reactions of the marketplace, it also can be costly and time-consuming and may lack validity and reliability.

GLOBAL MARKET INTELLIGENCE

The intensified global competition of the last two decades has put extreme pressure on the ability of organizations to gather reliable information about existing and potential global competitors. The relative wealth of information about markets within the United States has proven both advantageous to foreign competitors seeking access to the U.S. market and a competitive disadvantage to U.S. companies attempting to retain local market share. The success of European and Japanese entry into the U.S. market can be traced at least in part to this situation.

As we have already said, in the 1990s the United States will face fierce competition, not only from Japan and Germany but from the building economic powers of the EC, the impending boom in the Pacific Rim, and the emerging vitality among developing countries in Eastern Europe, Latin America, and the Middle East. This reality has caused and will continue to cause dramatic improvements in global marketing intelligence activities, supported by a vastly improved set of primary and secondary resources.

Gathering Global Market Intelligence

Recognizing the need for market intelligence, the U.S. Congress passed the Omnibus Trade Competitiveness Act of 1988, which requires the U.S. Department of Commerce to develop and maintain a data bank with information on foreign economies and export opportunities. Many other sources of global secondary market intelligence are available (some have already been mentioned in the section on electronic data base sources). Other sources include *MarketSearch, the International Directory of Published Market Research*, published annually and subject cross-referenced, and *Marketing Surveys Index (MSI)*, published ten times a year.

More generalized sources of global market information include *Croner's A-Z of Business Information Sources, Consumer Japan, Consumer Europe*, and "The Global 1,000," an annual issue of *Business Week* magazine. In addition, most countries publish indexes and directories on subjects related to business activity. *The Worldwide Government Directory* provides listings of governmental agencies around the globe.[1]

It is also possible to gather primary marketing intelligence. A number of companies and agencies exist in various parts of the world to assist in the gathering of primary data. Obtaining accurate information, however, can be tricky. Language and local customs can make it difficult to compare data, as can the fact that many countries use differing definitions and assumptions in compiling data. Also, outside agencies may lack experience in local environments, thus posing other serious problems.

As Europe standardizes statistics, definitions, and cooperation under the EC, the task of gathering MI there will become easier, as it will in Japan as marketers gain more experience. In Eastern Europe and other areas of the developing world, the task will remain risky, yet essential for the many companies seeking competitive success.

As we noted at the beginning of this chapter, seeking a competitive edge is every manager's job. The effective use of marketing intelligence is essential to achieving that objective. Nonmarketers need to understand the importance of this task and assist marketers in fulfilling this responsibility.

1. For a detailed listing of global sources of secondary marketing research and intelligence information, see: Ian MacFarlane, "Do-It-Yourself Marketing Research," *Management Review* (May 1991), pp. 34–37.

CHAPTER 4

Tools for Analyzing Market Intelligence

As we discussed in Chapter 3, gathering market intelligence consists of two activities: collecting and analyzing data. The previous chapter explored means of collecting data; this chapter covers analysis of data and applications of the results of such analysis.

Collections of marketing data generated by managers are often complicated and nebulous; they often include not only facts, which can be verified, but also opinions, which are not easily checked. Regardless of what a data collection contains, however, only when its contents are organized and analyzed can it yield the useful information managers need for planning.

The first task in analyzing a collection of raw data is to present it in a form that can be easily approached. This requires that accuracy be checked, facts and figures be classified in meaningful ways, and statistical arranging of numbers be performed so that the relationships between groups of data are as clear as possible.

After preparing the data, the manager applies the appropriate tools of analysis. These tools may be in the form of performance measurements in various areas of the operation, or they may be financial checks, such as return on investment or the break-even point. The results of the analyses are then used as guides in forecasting and budgeting, the basic prerequisites for preparing any strategic marketing plan.

The computer is a useful tool for storing quantities of data, analyzing them, and retrieving them in a usable format. A variety of spreadsheet programs, such as the popular Lotus 1-2-3, permits you to change one number and instantly observe the effects of that change on other numbers. Still other computer programs use pro forma statements, which represent financial projections of future company performance. Other computer-generated statistics from industry and government sources provide mountains of data on consumer price indexes, manufacturers' new orders and inventories, industrial production indexes, new housing starts, personal income, retail sales, and consumer installment credit. However, although the computer is capable of storing, manipulating, and retrieving information, there is still the vital human factor of a manager standing back from the maze of information, exercising business judgment, and asking, "With the aid of market intelligence, what should I be looking for?"

It's important to be specific about what you should analyze and what areas of the market/competitive situation you should be sensitive to, given the many possibilities open for examination. The dominant guideline for employing market intelligence is that the quality of the strategic marketing plan and the success in implementing the plan's strategies are only as good as the quality of market intelligence you input. The following case examples illustrate competitive problems faced by two companies, the strategies each pursued, and the MI factors and the tools of analysis used by each.

CASE EXAMPLE 1

Competitive Problem

Gillette Company managers faced a tough order from senior management after going through a major reorganization in 1990: increase profits. Cutting costs is one method of achieving this goal. But that approach by itself is overly simplistic. Instead, utilizing creative marketing strategy, managers found a major profit opportunity in exploiting a powerful asset: the Gillette brand name.

The Gillette product line includes such shaving products as Good News disposable razors and the highly rated Trac 11 and Ultra shaving systems. Analysis of the product line revealed that Gillette made three times more money on the cartridge refills for its reusable systems than on the disposables. However, further analysis showed that 40 percent of the dollars spent by men on shaving products goes for disposables. That was the problem—and the opportunity.

To improve profits, Gillette managers had two possibilities. The company had to capture ten percentage points of the U.S. market share from competitors—or persuade five million Good News customers to shift to its shaving systems. Managers decided to concentrate resources primarily on shaving systems. The following strategies both improved marketing productivity and increased Gillette's profits.

Gillette's Strategies

1. *Advertising strategy:* Management shifted virtually the entire advertising budget to shaving systems, compared to the former allocation of 70 percent to disposables. It assigned to advertising the formidable objective of convincing men that shaving systems give a shave worth twice the price of disposables.

MI factors: With Gillette's bold decision to concentrate almost its entire advertising budget on a single product line, MI had to measure the overall effectiveness of its advertising in converting men to its shaving systems. The analysis also had to detail geographical purchase patterns by types of retail outlets. Such information highlights market segments with the greatest potential for market share penetration and feeds the strategy-selection process by determining, for example, how to deploy the salesforce, where to increase in-store promotional displays, and when to develop additional merchandising programs.

Comparative research on competitive advertising campaigns would further assist in formulating strategies for determining which additional market segments to concentrate on. Organizations such as Starch and Gallup & Robinson, Inc., test ads placed in magazines; other research services conduct pre- and post-test research for print and broadcast campaigns.

2. *Distribution strategy:* Observing a gap in market coverage at grocery stores—an area of distribution they had not fully saturated— Gillette managers stepped up efforts to penetrate those outlets.

MI factors: A variety of intelligence activities are useful in executing distribution strategies, for example, evaluating the efficiency with which the product physically moves through the distribution channels to various retail outlets; measuring the responsiveness of retailers and consumers to in-store promotions and point-of-purchase displays; and determining through formal attitude research and personal interview what training or support would stimulate distributors and retailers to provide greater support to the product line. Also useful is feedback identifying what incentives would stimulate consumer purchases; assessing the ease of inventory control and reordering procedures; determining the frequency of out-of-stock occurrences; and probing for gaps in distribution coverage.

Competitors' activities on all these factors are also researched to permit side-by-side comparisons and to identify opportunities resulting from competitors' weaknesses.

3. *Brand expansion strategy:* Managers exploited the Gillette brand name by using it on related products, including shaving cream, after-shave lotion, and deodorant. The strategy increased the dollar volume for the company and for distributors and retailers.

MI factors: Extending the use of the brand name to related products has tremendous advantages for additional sales. Conversely, disadvantages exist in launching products that lack credibility in terms of what the brand stands for in the minds of consumers. MI measures the perception held by consumers; it determines if the brand's strength in its core product can carry over to related products or if its use for other products would damage the brand image. In addition, usage studies determine the frequency of usage of proposed new products.

4. *Product development strategy:* Managers launched an advanced line of shaving systems. Packages and promotions for its shaving and related products were standardized in all global markets, thereby building a "fortress" around the Gillette name and reducing costs.

MI factors: Ongoing MI is called for to implement this strategy; internally, from product developers and salespeople, and externally, from users, middlemen, and professional researchers. Specifically, MI should acquire data on new product acceptance, competitive product studies, packaging design, customer service, and any other areas related to competitive advantage.

CASE EXAMPLE 2

Competitive Problem

SmithKline Beecham is the result of a merger of the U.S.-based Smith-Kline Beckman Corporation and Britain's Beecham Group. The combination created a pharmaceutical organization powerful enough to meet competitive challenges that each alone could not meet.

The conditions triggering the merger are similar to those found among a variety of companies facing aggressive competitors. We now examine some of the conditions as they relate to MI.

Although Beecham's sales were a substantial $1.5 billion in 1990, the company was still too small to compete successfully with industry giants such as Merck, Bristol-Myers, Squibb, and Ciba-Geigy. It also was weak in two critical areas—maintaining a steady flow of new products and sustaining enough marketing power to penetrate target markets before generics are introduced, squeezing profits.

As for SmithKline, its record of new-product development left much to be desired. Even with heavy spending, it developed few new products over a ten-year period. Corporate sales were overly dependent on its well-known Tagamet ulcer drug. SmithKline also needed strengthening in market coverage, product development, and operational efficiencies.

SmithKline's Strategies

1. *Market strategy:* Markets were evaluated for long-term potential. Beecham is strong in Europe, SmithKline in the United States. Together, as SmithKline Beecham, the company hit global markets such as animal health, clinical testing labs, and over-the-counter drugs.

MI factors: To implement the strategy, the combined managements had to think globally but act locally. A global industry analysis would provide managers with such intelligence as total sales, economic conditions, market growth, demand for basic or state-of-the-art technology, and types of distribution networks. It would also permit isolating specific geographic areas for special attention. For instance, applying MI to a segmentation strategy could direct action at a target industry, such as animal health or clinical testing labs. Then, by classifying the total market as single market, multimarket, regional market, national market, or international market, precise tactical actions could be executed.

Sizeable amounts of secondary information are available from industry associations, libraries, and syndicated studies. Also available are primary research data accumulated by local distributors, sales representatives, customers, and technical personnel. Reliable intelligence related to this application assists in product formulation, packaging, pricing, technical service, promotion, and distribution.

2. *Product mix strategy:* New and existing products were evaluated not only for their market-by-market potential but for global competitiveness. An ambitious objective of two new products a year was established. (By comparison, one major competitor claimed that its six new products developed over ten years qualified as exceptional perfor-

mance.) Further, managing the product mix more efficiently permitted some of SmithKline's strong over-the-counter products, such as Contac, Tums, and Sucrets, to fund the increased R&D effort.

MI factors: Initiating new product acceptance studies along with competitive product studies can generate meaningful intelligence to assist marketing and nonmarketing managers in making decisions about how to protect existing business and seek growth opportunities. For example, *new product* studies would uncover opportunities for product developers to differentiate new products from competitive offerings, determine the marketability of a product, and assess the strengths and weaknesses of competitors' market presence.

Competitive product studies reveal opportunities to extend the life of *existing products* by determining if the product is reaching its intended audience, monitoring the product's present market position against competing products, and identifying declining niches worth exiting or emerging niches worth pursuing. These studies also identify opportunities for expanding product usage, determining potential for product-line extensions, or deciding where to prune the product line.

3. *Promotion strategy:* Unifying the salesforces created a 6,000-strong global sales group. The move resulted in more precise deployment of the combined salesforce against target markets.

MI factors: A variety of MI applications relate to this strategy. Market share analysis, sales analysis, sales territory reviews, sales compensation studies, and promotional studies of premiums, coupons, sampling, and deals provide the information to execute the strategy.

DISSEMINATING MARKET INTELLIGENCE

What can be learned from the foregoing cases? Consider the following points:

- MI must be *accurate*; critical decisions affecting expenditures of money, human resources, and time are at stake.
- MI must be *timely*; events have time cycles which, once past, may not occur again or whose opportunities are lost to competitors who have seized the moment.
- MI must be *usable*; data without a foundation for application become irrelevant. The foundation on which MI fits is the strategic marketing plan—with the provision, however, that the planning pro-

cess include the participation of marketing and nonmarketing personnel. As we have seen in the Gillette and SmithKline Beecham cases, MI impacts virtually all functions of the organization.

▪ MI must be *understandable*; information that cannot be internalized and interpreted with relative ease by the average manager and then applied to developing strategies and tactics is virtually useless. Avoid being tantalized by statistics and obscure phrases packaged to impress rather than formatted for comprehension.

▪ MI should be *meaningful*; if the information lacks importance, if it does not have sufficient significance but is merely nice-to-know information, the vital contribution of MI to the survival and growth of a business is missed.

Preparing and disseminating market intelligence in clear, discernible form is essential for good decision making. Preparation involves three steps: an appraisal of the data's accuracy, an arrangement of the data into proper classifications, and the presentation of the data to make comparisons easier.

Checking for Accuracy

With all the emphasis placed on the care needed in collecting data, it is important not to overlook the importance of accuracy, for to overlook that issue places any such project in jeopardy.

A check for accuracy at this point usually involves two areas. First, was the method of collection consistent with the objectives of the strategic marketing plan? Second, do a few of the verifiable facts and figures themselves check back accurately to their sources? If the proper collection methods were used and if the few random figures selected for source checking turn out to have been faithfully recorded, the manager can assume that the collection probably contains accurate data.

Consider, for example, how a particular collection of data used to survey wholesaler customers and containing Department of Commerce figures for a specific area was checked. To assess the accuracy of the data, the manager or researcher might have verified that questionnaires were sent to all the wholesaler customers, that a reasonable number of questionnaires were returned with sufficient answers to produce a valid sample of the group as a whole, that a half dozen of the most important figures recorded from the Department of Commerce were the most recent available, and that they were recorded without introducing error.

This point in the process is the last chance to review whether the raw data are reliable and representative. Reliable data can produce trustworthy and useful information, whereas mistakes in collecting and recording data will be perpetuated all the way through the data analysis and will result in distorted information that can mislead the manager and weaken the effectiveness of the plan.

Classifying the Data

After checking the raw data for accuracy, the manager must then arrange it according to whatever classifications permit the best analysis. The choice of classifications depends on the application of the analysis to planning.

Data collected about the transactions occurring in a particular store department for a given week could be classified by dollar amount of transactions, by number of items involved in transactions, by category of each item purchased, or by characteristics of the customers making the purchases. A manager setting up a work schedule for the department would classify the transactions according to the time they took place in order to staff the department to meet peaks in customer traffic; a manager interested in figuring out profitable future merchandise assortments probably would concentrate on the classification of transactions according to the category of item purchased.

Types of Classifications. Although it is possible to classify data in a great many ways, each classification falls within one of four basic types of classifications:

1. *Quantitative:* a classification of data by difference in amount, such as a classification of sales by number of units sold or number of transactions involved
2. *Qualitative:* a classification of data by difference in kind, such as a classification of sales by type of product sold, type of brand sold, or type of customer involved in sale
3. *Chronological:* a classification of data according to a time sequence, such as a classification of the average number of transactions handled during each hour of the working day
4. *Geographic:* a classification of data by difference in location, such as a classification of sales by store location, market area, or sales district

Mathematicians recognize two types of classifications of data: quantitative and qualitative. Chronological and geographic differences are considered either quantitative or qualitative. But to marketers, for whom timing and location are so important, chronological and geographic classifications are often ranked as separate and equal in importance to the two basic types recognized by the mathematical world.

Identification of Classifications. A classification usually takes the form of a table, chart, or graph. It is important that these displays be properly identified. The identification should include a definition of what the table, chart, or graph is about; an explanation of any unusual factors that influenced the findings; and an identification of the amount of data on which the table, chart, or graph is based.

For instance, a table of shoe sales classified by size of shoe could be very helpful in helping the store manager determine future inventory needs. But what if the table includes figures for both sports shoes and casual shoes? In order to analyze and understand the information, the manager has to know exactly which types of shoes are included in each category. If he doesn't know, he may stock his store with sneakers when what he really needs is more loafers. What if the data were amassed during the back-to-school period, a traditionally strong period for shoe sales? Unless the manager knows what type of shoe was sold and that the collection of data was made during that particular time period, he may find himself overstocked with school shoes but understocked for other kinds of styles during the winter and spring seasons.

What happens when the table represents only a small sampling of sales, such as a week's actual figures projected for an entire month, or when the sales were made to a small random sampling of customers? Small samplings sometimes point up situations that a manager might investigate, but only samplings large enough to represent the group as a whole can be considered reliable trend indicators.

Utilizing the Data

The final task of data preparation is using the data to make relationships meaningful. This task involves applying specific statistical techniques to the data so that they can be analyzed more easily. The most common kinds of utilization involve working out statistics such as averages, medians, percentages, and ratios.

A ratio is the relationship between two figures reduced to the form of a divisor and a dividend. Stockturn, which is the number of times an average inventory of stock is sold during a given period of time, is usually expressed as a ratio. Products that move rapidly, such as canned food, may have stockturn ratios of 10:1 or 12:1 per month, which means that the basic stock carried by the market sells, is replaced, and is resold ten or twelve times during a given month. In contrast, fine jewelry may have stockturn ratios more in the neighborhood of 2:1 or lower in a six-month period, which indicates that the items involved earned only two sales or fewer during that period.

In addition to underlining relationships between figures and making figures easier to analyze, utilization often results in condensing data in what otherwise would be a very long table. Instead of having fifty-two weekly totals in a table that shows sales for a year, perhaps a single weekly average or median figure for each selling season or distinctive sales period could serve much the same purpose. As long as the summary or condensed figures are representative of the original groups of figures, they can simplify and speed up the analysis. Here, too, as in the other areas of classifying data, computer software makes the job easier.

PERFORMANCE ANALYSIS

The analysis of data usually involves a series of separate individual analyses, each designed to explore one particular facet of the data. Thus, a collection of sales figures might be analyzed by types of items sold as well as by points of market share and in terms of gross margin as well as selling costs.

A manager usually needs two kinds of data as an aid in making decisions. She needs general operating data to help in normal business planning and special data to support decisions concerning specific problems or opportunities. Because the creation of general operating data is a regular and continuing process, the analyses of these data are most frequently performed by the marketer. The most basic of the analyses performed on general data involve calculations based on performance records such as sales, market share, distribution, profit and cost, and the salesforce.

How frequently such analyses are made depends completely on the kind of business that is involved. A manager of a small business or one handling a very stable product may not need to check performance records more than monthly or quarterly and may not need to make any particularly detailed analyses more than quarterly or seasonally. On the other hand, a manager who is responsible for a variety of products or who handles highly volatile products needs to keep much closer track of performance records. Sometimes the entire market picture can change unexpectedly within a week or two, and that change could require immediate action by the manager.

Sales Analysis

A good sales analysis shows more than the developments in total sales volume. It also helps the manager pinpoint weaknesses and strengths in the sales picture as they occur. This kind of analysis should do the following:

1. Classify sales by product or category.
2. Provide a profile of the customer by demographics and by time and place of purchase (optional depending on type of business, but used increasingly at computerized retail checkout stations, particularly where credit cards are used).
3. Add up unit and dollar totals.
4. Compare totals with previous periods' figures and budgeted figures to determine whether results are behind, even with, or ahead of expectations.

The key to success is making sure that the sales figures are divided according to classifications that the manager finds beneficial. Depending upon the kind of business involved, a manager may need two classifications or one hundred classifications, ranging from geographic region to type of product; regardless of the number of categories, only when the figures are divided into meaningful groups are the results of the sales analysis useful as a planning and a control tool.

In recent years, many larger industries have had to rethink their entire classification system. In strongly competitive markets where customer-oriented marketing is practiced with increasing levels of sophistication, it is important that managers plan on the basis of customer problems and needs, customer buying patterns, demographics, and buying behavior profiles.

The demand for detailed data has been a particular problem for larger companies because of the quantity of data required for a good sales analysis. However, new computer systems and software help managers to collect, prepare, and analyze the volume of sales data that today's competitive markets demand. Systems and software can be customized to accommodate the particular requirements of a company; increasingly, industry publications and trade associations are advertising the availability of either generic or industry-specific software.

Market Share Analysis

Those companies large enough to figure sales based on their share of the total market usually need some sort of market share analysis. In a way, a market share analysis is a test of the sales figures. A 10 percent increase in sales may look healthy, but how healthy is it if the size of the total market has increased 20 percent during the same period? Such results may mean the company's share of market has not increased or even held even but has actually decreased in relation to its competitors. A share-of-the-market analysis is computed by first determining total market sales by dollars and units; next, determining company sales by dollars and units; and, finally, establishing the percentage of company sales in relation to total market sales.

While a manager can obtain company sales figures from within the company, a share-of-the-market analysis also requires figures collected from outside the company—from external sources. If a manager decides to collect market share figures, expensive and lengthy research in many fields may be required. However, in those areas in which companies are interested in market share analysis, reports are often available from various syndicated data firms, as well as from government agencies, trade associations, and industry publications. Obtaining data on a regular basis may be expensive; the cost is based on the type and availability of market share data desired. For example, data on market share can be acquired on the following:

1. Overall market share for a product category
2. Market share figures for a specific market segment or product application
3. Data on a group of competitors that account for the majority of product or segment sales
4. Market share relative to a specific competitor

In some fields, a steady flow of data about changing market statistics may cost a company upward of several thousand dollars a month; for companies that plan in terms of market share, such information is well worth the price.

Companies that can benefit from market share analysis are those with a measurable share of one of the big consumer markets and with a high stockturn rate. In such markets, where there is a frequent shuffling of product preferences, customer loyalty, customer demand, and price sensitivity, a manager must continually adjust operations to meet these changes or else lose valuable business.

While market share analysis provides the figures, human insight is needed to determine the reasons for significant ups or downs in numbers. Did the competing company's share of market rise dramatically because of aggressive strategies to "buy" market share at any cost, or was that company acquired by another, providing an inflow of funds? Conversely, did a competing company's share drop because of a need for greater profit margins regardless of market share loss, because of a change in the company's strategy requiring retrenchment, or, perhaps, because of a shift in the strategic direction of the company away from the market in question? As in all areas of MI analysis, managers must look for the reasons behind the numbers. Determining the reasons provides the critical ingredient needed for developing countermeasures in the form of competitive strategies.

Distribution Analysis

A distribution analysis concentrates on the channels of distribution and the physical movement of the products to the customers. There is no set formula or method of procedure; each company must determine what information it needs and then collect and analyze that information regularly. Typical information includes:

- Type, size, and location of outlet
- Sales of company's products generated by outlet and in units, dollars, net profits, and total sales made by outlet (if possible)
- Inventory carried by outlet
- Shipments made to outlet, receipts acknowledged by outlet, average time stock remains in outlet

Other analysis might include:

- Assessing productivity of manual inventory control systems compared with computerized systems such as EDI (Electronic

Data Interchange)—for your company, for competitors, for the industry
- Assessing effectiveness of market coverage with warehouse locations
- Assessing efficiencies of transportation modes related to on-time delivery
- Assessing effectiveness of channel members: distributors, dealers, manufacturers' representatives, brokers, agents; assessing any shift in power in the distribution channel in which one channel member displaces another in ability to dictate terms, procedures, or standards of performance

With such information, a manager can not only determine which outlets are doing the best job with the company's products but point out possible weaknesses or trouble spots in the distribution network, such as delays in delivering shipments to an outlet or the beginning of an unusually heavy inventory buildup in a particular outlet. Managers use the distribution analysis both to control current operations and to plan future ones. When a trouble spot appears, it can be investigated and corrected. When a channel of distribution or a form of physical handling of a product shows unusual success, the reasons can be identified; if the method seems workable and affordable and if it serves a competitive advantage, it can be the basis for a new distribution strategy.

Most of the required data are in the customer records and the sales and audit reports supplied by the outlets. Whatever else is needed can be collected on a regular basis from channel members and by the market intelligence techniques cited in Chapter 3.

Profit and Cost Analysis

Even if the sales figures look healthy, the share-of-market figures look satisfactory, and the distribution analysis doesn't show any problems, the company's financial capability to respond to competitive threats can be at risk. This can be true for the company as a whole, for one particular division within the company, or for one product or group of products. An analysis of profit and cost tells the story.

There are several ways that profit and cost figures are collected and analyzed. These include the gross margin system, the natural expense system, and the functional cost system.

Gross Margin. A gross margin system of profit and cost account-ing compares all cost allocated to a department, category, or product classification with the gross profit indicated by the margin percentage. Here is the calculation:

$$\text{Gross Margin \%} - \text{Total Costs \%} = \text{Profit \%}$$

This basic departmental analysis, however, can leave some prob-lems and opportunities undiscovered. Marketers with a variety of products and a number of selling departments should try to develop profit and cost analyses for the major product classifications. This can be hard to do at times, both because it requires collecting considerable data and because some general departmental costs are hard to divide among the various products carried in the department. However, only a detailed analysis by major product lines or classifications can show the marketer which products are the strong profit producers and which products are not profit producers.

Natural Expense. The natural expense system is the standard method of business accounting. Costs are divided into three broad groups—materials, labor, and overhead—and then into various subgroups. Profit is the percentage of income earned in excess of these costs. Although this method of figuring is generally valid for all kinds of businesses, the three standard classifications of costs are not always appropriate for all kinds of businesses.

A large organization, for instance, may assign office floor space and then charge each division for the space in accordance with the number of employees and the jobs they perform. For department stores, however, the amount of sales per square foot of selling space earned by each department is a major factor in determining how much space to assign a department and what to charge it.

Functional Cost. The functional cost system attempts to assign all costs incurred by the company to a particular product or project. These costs are then compared with the income produced by that product or project, and the result is the amount of profit produced. The basic formula is similar to that of the gross margin system:

$$\text{Income} - \text{Costs} = \text{Profit}$$

Or, in terms of planning:

$$\text{Planned Profit} = \text{Planned Income} - \text{Planned Costs}$$

When planned figures are not matched by actual results, the manager has to make adjustments to keep operations in balance. The danger of a planned drop-off in profit or income is obvious. But unexpected increases in expenses may mean that some function requires improvement and that sales figures may eventually be affected if the change is not made.

A functional cost analysis is perhaps the most useful kind of profit and cost calculation, but it can be hard to figure. For instance, it is relatively easy to calculate or record the cost of manufacturing and shipping a product, but it is far more complicated to estimate the costs of product development and improvement and then allocate them accurately among the different stages of the product's expected life cycle.

Salesforce Analysis

An important way of checking the efficiency of the salesforce is by analyzing its selling cost as a percentage of sales volume for a particular period, typically, a month, a season, or a year. Here is the formula:

$$\$ \text{ Sales Volume} \div \$ \text{ Salesforce Expense} = \% \text{ Salesforce Expense}$$

The sales volume may equal the total sales income of the entire company, a single department, a sales district within the company, or a product or category of products. Similarly, the salesforce cost may be costs incurred by the company's entire selling staff, by salespeople within one department of a sales district, or by each individual salesperson. Retailers usually analyze selling force expense by total company sales in a small operation and by department sales in larger operations; manufacturers, wholesalers, and industrial marketers often analyze selling expense by sales district, by individual salesperson, and by product or product category.

When individual sales performance is vital to a marketer, as it is in any operation that depends heavily on the salesforce to do the largest part of the selling job, then such an analysis usually includes, in addition to the basic data in the formula, the following information:

- Unit sales made by each salesperson

- Expenses incurred by each salesperson
- Gross margin earned by each salesperson
- Number of calls made per day
- Number of new accounts obtained
- Number of existing customers lost
- Amount of time spent in nonselling duties
- Percentage of orders per one hundred sales calls

This analysis permits the manager to pinpoint which salespeople by sales area are contributing the most net profit to the company, which salespeople are finding the most new contacts for the company, which work patterns seem to be the most effective, and which salespeople are contributing most to achieving strategic marketing planning objectives. Such an analysis requires the preparation and checking of percentages and ratios, by individual salespeople, sales districts, or selling departments. It also compares planned goals with the figures for the company as a whole, as well as with competitors' results. In this way, both weaknesses and strengths in the selling force can be identified, the strong rewarded, and the weak, if possible, trained and encouraged to improve performance.

FINDING THE FINANCIAL STRUCTURE

Performance analysis both serves as a means of checking progress and provides data for future planning and decision making. Some of the results of performance analysis affect two critical types of financial figuring—the analysis of return on investment and the break-even analysis. Both are used to project as accurately as possible what the data mean for future balance sheets.

Return on investment, or ROI, can be used to study the company as a whole or to study a particular project or product. Calculating ROI requires plotting the total cost investment throughout the life of a product or project and then figuring the return that investment will earn for the company.

The break-even analysis is primarily a test of future product profitability. The product may already be on the market, or it may still be in its earliest planning stages. The analysis explores the relationship among cost, price, and sales volume, determining where the break-even point in profit would logically occur in each possible combination of these factors. Managers use break-even analysis to determine at what specific combination of cost, price, and sales volume the product may be expected to begin to turn profits.

Return on Investment

Every dollar spent on marketing must eventually pay off in an acceptable return on that investment to the company. It isn't enough that an investment merely produce a profit. That profit must be great enough, in terms of a percentage of the original investment, so that the company not only survives but is financially healthy enough to compete and prosper.

An ROI calculation does not guarantee success. Conditions in any market can change too rapidly and too radically for such predictions to be reliable. However, a good ROI analysis does reduce the risks and guesswork of decision making. It can be used both to gauge the rate of return an investment is earning and to estimate what return will be earned during a future period by a specific investment. Thus, it is the one form of analysis that takes into consideration the effect of time on the cost of money.

Gauging an Investment. Whether a manager wants to analyze a past investment, a current investment, or a possible future investment, the basic steps in figuring its rate of return are approximated the same:

1. List all the assets involved.
2. Figure the profit earned by those assets during the relevant period of time.
3. Figure the investment turnover for the same period of time.
4. Multiply the percentage of profit earned by the rate of turnover. The result is the rate of return on the investment for the specified period.

For instance, a company may have two sales districts with identical sales figures, identical expense figures, and therefore identical profit figures. Yet the districts may be quite different in terms of inventory carried and receivables outstanding. Therefore, the company may decide to do an ROI analysis on each sales district to determine which one is doing a better job with the company's money, as shown in Table 4-1. Although sales and expenses may be the same, producing the same profits on paper, district A is using a larger investment than

Table 4-1. ROI comparison of two sales districts.

CALCULATION	DISTRICT A	DISTRICT B
1. Sales	$200,000	$200,000
2. Cost of goods sold	−110,000	−110,000
3. Gross margin	90,000	90,000
4. Marketing costs	−30,000	−30,000
5. Net income	$ 60,000	$ 60,000
6. Accounts receivable	24,000	50,000
7. Inventories	66,000	20,000
8. Total investment	$ 90,000	$ 70,000
9. Profit on sales (profit margin) (line 5 ÷ line 1)	30%	30%
10. Investment (line 1 ÷ line 8)	2.2 times	2.9 times
11. Return on investment (line 9 × line 10)	66%	87%

district B to produce those results. This means that district B is earning a better return on investment than district A.

Discounting the Cash Flow. Money costs money. If you borrow $1,000, you will owe interest on that money each day until it is paid back. In accounting terms, interest, or the cost of money, "discounts" the full amount back to the amount borrowed.

An investment is a form of loan made by the company to the product or project. When a manager figures what return an investment may produce in a future period, such as the next five years, a standard compound interest table is used to figure the actual cost of the money involved in that investment. The total assets invested each year are multiplied by the cost of the money or interest rate to determine total financial investment. Then total expenses are deducted. The result is the projected net profit or net cash flow generated by the investment.

By using a calculation that takes into account the effect of time to estimate future return on an investment, a manager can figure what rate of interest will discount the net cash flow for each future year back to the original compounded cost of the investment. This calculation involves the use of a value table that charts amounts and rate of discount for each year into the future. Unless a manager has a financial background, this activity is usually handled by the accounting or financial department. However, it is useful for managers to have an understanding of the concept.

Break-Even Analysis

A break-even analysis helps managers answer such questions as "What profits will a specific product earn at various levels of sales volume?" "If the fixed costs of producing my product go up, what increase in sales volume will I need to maintain the same profit level?" and "What effect will a 10 percent decrease in sales have on the profit level?"

The relationships between cost, profit, and sales volume are explored by a break-even analysis. If a product is sold for a specific price, then a series of relationships exists between the number of units, the amount it will cost to produce them, and the profit they will earn. These relationships are usually calculated by mathematical formulas and are then pictured in chart or graph form. The mathematics produces the results of the analysis, while the chart or graph helps dramatize those results.

Analysis. The *break-even point* is the amount of income or sales volume needed to produce income equal to costs. Lower income or sales volume produces a loss, for costs exceed profits. Higher income or sales volume yields a net profit, for income more than covers costs, as shown in Figure 4-1. The formula for calculating the break-even point is:

$$\text{Break-Even Point} = \frac{\text{Fixed Costs}}{\text{Ratio of Gross Margin to Sales}}$$

Suppose a manager is considering adding a new line that is expected to produce the following figures:

	Dollars	Percent of Net Sales
Net sales	$100,000	100
Variable costs	−40,000	−40
Gross margin	60,000	60
Fixed costs	−30,000	−30
Net operating profit	$ 30,000	30

Figure 4-1. Break-even chart.

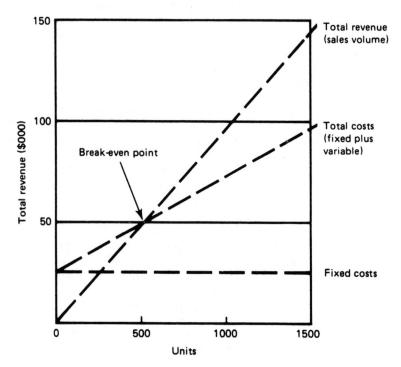

Fixed costs are estimated at $30,000, and the ratio of gross margin to net sales is 60 percent. The formula then reads:

$$\frac{\$30,000}{60\%} = \text{Break-Even Point, or } \$50,000$$

The Variables. The formula and the tabulation are worked out on the basis of a set price or series of prices to be charged for the product line. Different prices produce different results. In the same way, changing any of the elements—price, sales volume, or fixed costs—changes the equation and the break-even point.

The manager can experiment with a variety of combinations that produce the desired results. Then, with the summary of relationships, the manager can track how changes in those elements affect the over-all profit and cost picture.

SOME PITFALLS IN ANALYSIS

Whether the analysis of marketing data is done by a trained researcher in a large organization or handled by a small-shop owner, there are some pitfalls that should be avoided. The trained researcher may be more aware of these dangers than the shop owner, but both can learn from some of the don'ts of analysis.

1. *Don't set out to produce startling results.* There is a temptation to try to read big news into what are relatively commonplace results. There is also a temptation to bias the results of an analysis slightly to make the results seem different or interesting. A manager does not need something unusual for planning; instead, she needs solid and reliable deductions.

2. *Don't be swayed by favorable evidence, and don't ignore adverse data.* Often a manager hopes that analyses will produce particular results. He wants figures that show that sales are healthy, that a new product is producing a reasonable profit, or that certain new equipment would be a wise investment. In an attempt to have the figures show what the manager wants them to show, an analysis may be skewed, intentionally or unintentionally, to give prominence to favorable evidence, with adverse data somehow getting lost in the shuffle. This may make the results appear more optimistic, but those results are just the product of wishful thinking, not a groundwork on which prudent decisions can be built.

3. *Don't get fascinated by details.* The value of an analysis is that it interprets and simplifies the original data. The whole purpose of an analysis is to produce summary information out of raw bulk details. Therefore, keep the results of each analysis as simple as possible, and do not let any analysis develop into a mass of statistics.

4. *Don't project from samples that are too small.* Some managers enjoy playing with figures, and at times they have a tendency to draw remarkable inferences from a very few pieces of data. While significant information should be recognized and noted, even when based on a small number of cases, it should not have its importance magnified out of proportion. Further, if insufficient data are available about a particular subject, then those data have to be flagged with the warning that the results are based on an insufficient sampling.

5. *Don't mistake opinion for fact.* Some data are verifiable; some aren't. Managers work with both types. In some cases, however, the

data must be fact, not opinion; substituting opinion for fact may lead to trouble later.

6. *Don't put too much faith in averages.* While averages can be useful, they are only a handy tool, not an accurate summation of figures. If the customers of a gasoline station drive an average of one-third of a sports car per family, it does not mean that every family has an equal interest in sports cars. What it does mean is that there are enough sports cars owned by customers for the station manager to consider stocking a restricted line of special accessories.

7. *Don't confuse cause with effect.* Did the drop in dollar sales volume cause the increase in markdowns taken, or were the markdowns taken too early, causing the drop in dollar sales volume? Did sales of a particular line improve because a new distribution channel was chosen, or was a new distribution channel chosen because sales had improved? Misreading cause and effect can damage the validity of an analysis, which can create problems. The lesson: When interpreting data, question, probe, and investigate until the results of the analyses make sense.

FORECASTING

The results of data analysis are the tools managers use to handle their competitive problems and market opportunities. Specifically, the manager uses the data to forecast future conditions as they relate to products, technology, markets, and competition. The job of forecasting is not a mechanical process, nor is it subject to the same kind of precise rules of mathematics as the analysis of data. Indeed, it requires a blend of:

- *Objectivity:* the ability to keep one's own biases and prejudices separate from what the data show
- *Realism:* the ability to see both the problems and opportunities clearly and to select the information that will be most useful in making correct decisions about those problems and opportunities
- *Competent use of formal logic:* a base for all forecasting that keeps the manager from making mistakes in interpreting what she knows and sees
- *Business sense:* the ability to make decisions based on educated

guesswork—the kind of guesswork that is backed by all the information available, common sense, and a firm grasp of the business of marketing

Forecasting is a vital part of planning. Without a forecast of what can happen, no manager can work out plans for the future. Without a plan, a manager can merely react, not act, and will always be a little behind the competition, always in some danger of being edged out of business by a more farsighted competitor.

Timing

It takes accurate data analysis to produce good forecasts, but it also takes forecasting to produce the data needed for an analysis. Analysis that projects performance into the future, such as return-on-investment and break-even analysis, can be useful in overall forecasting for the company or the market.

For example, a performance analysis may show that sales in a particular market segment are rising. A manager may take the results of this analysis, add more data, and project sales for that segment for the next three years. That forecast may be used in an ROI analysis to determine whether increasing sales are going to increase the return on investment in that district. The ROI analysis, in turn, may show that the rate of return may weaken, because the increased demand for the product will cause a sharp rise in the expense of supplying that demand. Finalizing the sales forecasts before planning the company's investment could designate that particular segment as a possible problem area rather than an area of opportunity.

Methods

Managers have a variety of forecasting techniques at their disposal:

1. *Expert opinion.* This technique requires asking experts such as industry consultants, distributors, suppliers, and industry associations for their opinions on future trends. In addition, managers can consult industry forecasts available from such highly regarded economic forecasting firms as Wharton Econometric, Data Resources, and Chase Econometric.

2. *Group discussion.* This approach relies on a group of specialists

invited to participate in forecasting. Often, the team meets as a committee and comes up with a group estimate through consensus. The group discussion method has the advantage of merging divergent viewpoints and moderating individual biases. However, it is valuable to have a moderator guard against the possibility of one or more individuals dominating the group and forcing a point of view on others.

3. *Pooled individual estimates.* In this technique, a project leader simply merges separately supplied estimates into a single estimate without any interplay with or among the participants, thereby avoiding the potential pitfall of group dynamics.

4. *Delphi technique.* This technique overcomes any drawbacks of the group methods already described. Group members are asked to submit individual estimates and assumptions. These estimates are reviewed by the project leader, revised on the basis of the leader's tabulation of results and spotting of weaknesses in the first design, and fed back to the participants for a second round of individual estimating. During each round, participants are given the median forecast level that emerged from the previous round. Because the technique relies on written, rather than oral, communication, domination, undue conservatism, and argument are eliminated, even while the group members benefit from each other's input. After successive rounds of estimating and feedback, the process ends when a consensus emerges.

5. *Jury of executive opinion.* A jury of executive opinion is often composed of top-level personnel from various key functions such as sales, production, or finance. The major advantage of this group composition is that because those involved are working directly with each other, forecasts can be arrived at quickly. This advantage is, however, easily outweighed by the disadvantage inherent in involving people in the estimating process who, in spite of their high rank, are relatively unfamiliar with the forces that shape marketing success.

6. *Composite of salesforce opinion.* This approach collects product, customer, and/or territorial estimates from individual salespeople in the field who, since they are in constant contact with customers, should be in a position to predict buying plans and needs. They may even be able to take probable competitive activity into account. To counter the potential problem of salespeople's unfamiliarity with broad economic trends, many companies supply their salesforce with basic economic assumptions to guide their estimates.

7. *Test marketing.* Whereas the above techniques are for the most

part judgmental, test marketing entails introducing a new product or varying some component of the marketing mix (for example, promotion, price, or distribution) in a limited number of cities. The marketing program contemplated for national introduction is put into effect, scaled down to the local level but otherwise identical in every detail, including advertising, pricing, and packaging.

The effective analysis of marketing intelligence is essential to the marketer's ability to measure, evaluate, and project various scenarios. Nonmarketers are responsible for most of the tasks associated with the analysis. A clear understanding of the importance of these data plays a key role in fostering their ultimate usefulness to the company.

CHAPTER 5

Interpreting Clues to Consumer Behavior

Basic to the marketing-driven approach to doing business is the recognition that the best product or service offered for sale is the one that customers want to buy. For that reason, we have devoted two chapters to discussing marketing intelligence gathering and analysis.

However, it is important for nonmarketers to realize that the degree to which marketers can anticipate and interpret the pressures and influences on consumers—the practical aspects of why consumers react to certain presentations better than others and the elements that affect purchasing behavior—are equally important. Yet few aspects of marketing are more complex or elusive than those associated with consumer behavior. This chapter focuses on the nature and complexity of each individual and organizational purchasing decision, a topic known as *consumer behavior*.

Our task here is to introduce concepts and elements, show their respective value to the analysis, and give examples of how they are used by marketers, with the goal of giving nonmarketers an increased appreciation of the complexities of assessing and affecting the purchasing process. If nothing else, what follows will assist the reader to understand why it is that particular appeals are made in advertising, why some seemingly good products fail while others succeed, and why marketers spend so much time in luncheons, at trade shows, and talking to what sometimes seem to be the "wrong" people while doing their job.

The chapter is divided into two categories: *ultimate consumer purchasing behavior*—the behavior of each of us when purchasing products or services for our own personal use (also called "consumer behavior")—and *organizational purchasing behavior*—the behavior of industry, government, and other formal organizations when purchasing products and services to be used in doing business (also called "organizational buying behavior"). Both types of customers are affected by many of the same influences and pressures, but in different measure and in different ways. The different impact of the various influences is important enough for us to separate the two types of customers for our discussion as well as for marketing use in general.

CONSUMER BEHAVIOR

Consumer behavior analysis studies those elements that come into play when purchases are made for our use as individual consumers. In this case, the purchase of products or services is being guided by individual wants and desires, since the products will be used by us for our own satisfaction and use.

Definition of Consumer Behavior

Consumer behavior is the study of activities people go through in making purchasing decisions and the influences, emotions, and values involved in the process. The term "purchasing" in this context is not limited to a physical possession of a product; it also includes the purchase and use of services and the recognition and acceptance of related ideas and images.

The study of consumer behavior rests on the behavioral sciences, each of which makes a contribution to the theory. Our discussion draws on anthropology, psychology, social psychology, and sociology; while we separate the contributions of each discipline for the sake of clarity, it is important to remember that it is in the combination of these disciplines that the maximum value to marketing is derived.

The behavioral sciences of economics and demographics are interwoven into so many of the aspects of the marketing task and are discussed in so many other sections of this book that they are not presented in separate sections here. Economic theory is incorporated into discussion of subjects such as consumption, pricing, supply and demand; demographic elements are considered in our discussion of factors relating to age, education, household size, income, marital status, race, and sex.

Rational vs. Emotional Motives. Some products are unimportant to us, and our purchasing decisions are guided by factors such as price, availability, convenience of purchase, and durability. Such factors are sometimes labeled *rational motives*. The more consumers rely on these motives, the harder the marketing task of influencing customers to pass up a competitor's product. When rational purchasing considerations play key roles in purchasing behavior, marketers try to place their products as conveniently as possible and charge as low a price as possible. This simply reflects their recognition that to do otherwise would reduce sales. The vast majority of consumer purchasing decisions have some element of rational motivation, but not exclusively.

At other times, factors such as prestige, feelings of love, hate, fear, and pride, and emulation—factors labeled *emotional motives*—are important. The greater the degree to which emotional considerations can be brought to bear, the greater the opportunity for the marketer to obtain loyalty and repeat sales of a product and the greater the marketer's freedom to separate the price charged for a product from its cost.

The extent to which each of these sets of motives plays a role in a purchasing decision is complex. Generally, their relative weight is governed by the intensity of feeling and frustration generated by the consumer need, the sense of the importance of the purchase, and the ability to find acceptable choices.

The Consumer Purchasing Decision Process

Marketers have learned that most consumers either make a purchase decision promptly or go through an organized thought process to make their decision. In the first instance, the consumer is only moderately interested in the product and is comfortable that she knows enough to purchase successfully. This is sometimes called "routinized" behavior; the repurchase of regular items fall into this class, as do a whole set of impulse purchases, typically those from which consumers wish to obtain immediate pleasure, reward, or escape. To appeal to such purchasers, marketers of entertainment and pleasure items such as movies, video stores, and restaurants feature large displays, loud music, or flashing lights to attract the attention of potential customers as they pass by.

If they are uncertain about what they want and whether to make a purchase decision, consumers typically proceed through a formal decision process in which they:

- *Recognize a problem* which they believe they can solve through the purchase of some product or service.

- *Initiate a search for information* to clarify the type of product desired. One may simply recall a brand purchased in the past or seek assistance through the marketplace by asking others, reading ads, watching displays, or initiating more formal research. The intensity of the search is partly dependent on the consumer's "perceived risk" in making a decision, especially when none of the alternatives appear to provide complete satisfaction.

- *Assess the alternatives* available through product comparison, questioning others who seem to be "in the know" and continuing the direct comparison of alternative products on a number of sometimes competing bases. By this point in the search, the consumer is weighing many considerations, including how others will view this purchase and what losses will occur from not making particular alternate choices.

- *Make a purchase decision,* assuming the original need persists and a conscious process of comparison has continued. Typically, once a person becomes actively involved in comparison shopping, a momentum builds, leading to resolution of the consumer's frustration by the purchase of the perceived solution.

- *Undertake a postpurchase evaluation.* Once the purchase decision has been made, the consumer compares the expected solution with the reality of the result. If the consumer is satisfied, the product will have a loyal customer, one who will make future purchases of the same product, reflecting a "brand loyalty." If, as sometimes happens, the customer's satisfaction is less than expected, the customer will reject that product for future consideration, carrying a "negative image" of it from that point on.

Advertisers aim their presentations at one or more of these stages. For example, many ads try to assist consumers in identifying the problem their product can solve. A particular soap will "brighten dingy clothes"; a particular type of skin abrasion is identified and a product indicated "to cure it instantly." Other ads draw direct comparisons with competitive products. Tylenol, Nuprin, and Bayer Aspirin each tell of their particular ability to cure headaches more safely, more quickly, or more effectively than the identified competitors' products.

Still other ads focus on postpurchase confusion, frequently called "cognitive dissonance," in which consumers who are not completely satisfied are given reinforcement that they made the right purchase decision. Leading brands have a big stake in such reinforcement, so they spend a large portion of their energy on "taste" or "feel better" tests reminding existing customers how well their products perform. Although the comparison tests are constantly changed, each aims to reinforce the satisfaction to be derived from the promoted products.

A Three-Level Focus on Consumer Behavior

Each of our purchasing decisions is affected to a greater or lesser degree by many forces and influences, both rational and emotional. They are also influenced by such issues as our own feeling of independence or rebellion, as opposed to our interest in being viewed as a member of a particular group. Our decisions are also affected by our life style and our culture.

For our purposes, we will break the study of consumer behavior into three broad categories or levels, with the focus moving from the personal to interpersonal and then to encompassing influences.

Personal Influences. Personal influences, such as motivation, perception, learning, personality, and attitude, are important personal factors identified by psychologists and used by the marketer. Psychological mechanisms such as rationalization and projection can be brought into play.

Perception, the concept of "selective reality," is based on the manner in which our brain filters, sorts, and stores information. Psychologists have long recognized that the brain tries to find shortcuts to deal with the mass of information provided it. For example, when a person views a product or an idea, his brain not only receives information about the object but places a value on that information based on previous experience, the nature or circumstance under which the information was provided, and dozens of other filters. This filtered sense of a situation becomes the "real" or "perceived" (remembered) situation unless additional evidence is provided later on. So, an ad with four happily chatting white teenagers wearing a particular style of clothes will be perceived (observed and remembered) differently by other white teenagers than by black or Asian teenagers.

Our perceptions are influenced by our experiences in similar situations, our feelings about products or situations, and our attitudes
about the way in which a presentation is made. Thus, hunters retain
a different message from a demonstration of the effectiveness of a
particular type of gun than do city people worried about their safety.
Teenagers "hear" a different message in a discussion on the high-
speed performance of motorcycles than do older people, and ciga-
rette smokers derive a different sensory experience than do non-
smokers from the aroma of cigars.

Perception can also be built around one's interpretation of a
word. Allegheny Airlines found it much easier to be perceived as a
large, complex national airline once it changed its name to USAir. In
the same way, Kentucky Fried Chicken changed its name to KFC to
reduce the impact of the word "fried" during a period of changes in
customer eating habits.

To help create a positive perception of their products, marketers
frequently seek endorsements from popular celebrities. The hope is
that consumers will transfer their positive feeling and respect for the
celebrity to the product. On the other hand, an endorsement of a
product by a controversial celebrity is likely to leave a far different
impression, depending on the mental filter already in place. (It is for
this reason that a celebrity ad is so quickly removed if the sports figure
in it is accused of using drugs.) An instructive illustration along similar lines occurred with Domino's Pizza, one of the largest fast-food
purveyors in the United States. The president of Domino's decided to
give a significant contribution to an antiabortion group and was sur-
prised to find pro-choice advocates picketing at a number of his estab-
lishments, resulting in a drop in sales.

Proportionally many more black men wear hats than do white
men when they dress up, reflecting different feelings or perceptions
about hats. This results in different mental images for each group of
what being dressed up means. An ad for hats in a newspaper aimed
at black men can stress style; an ad in a paper aimed at white men
would be more likely to stress good health, for a hat might not be
considered stylish. Along the same lines, a young adult perceives a
three-year-old car as being a "newer" product than does his father.
Recognizing the importance of selective perception, many marketers
plan entirely different advertising campaigns for white audiences,
black audiences, and Hispanic audiences; much money is spent on
essentially redundant advertising as marketers attempt to get their
message through consumers' perception barriers.

Providing Desirable Sensory Cues. Creating sensory cues is one technique used by marketers to draw attention and to provide reinforcement to potential customers of some products. Cars and roses get the smell reinforcement test; foods get the correct color and taste test.

IFF (International Flavors and Fragrances), Quest International, and Universal Flavor Corporation are three of the largest companies in a growing business devoted to meeting the sensory expectations of consumers. Such companies concoct the fragrances for perfumes and provide artificial replacements to overcome product modifications that reduce fragrance and taste.

For example, taking the fat and sugar out of products also takes out much of the flavor. These companies have found a market in providing artificial flavors for foods that lose much of their natural flavor in processing. IFF provided McDonald's with a beef-fat flavor for its new low-cholesterol french fries, after McDonald's felt compelled to respond to pressures to stop preparing the product in animal fat. Similarly, it provides fragrance spray used by florists to compensate for the reduced natural aroma of roses produced with greater attention to color and size than to scent. A discreet application several times a day and during wrapping achieves the desired result.

IFF also provides new and used car dealerships with a spray to make sure that cars in their showrooms retain that unique vinyl/leathery smell so characteristic of new cars to many consumers. By using this spray, dealers compensate for the loss of scent that occurs when cars spend a long time in transit and on the back lot and when their doors and windows are opened frequently on the showroom floor. IFF also manufactures color formulas and dyes used by food processors in many fruits, juices, and other foods to overcome variations in crops and varieties and to match consumer expectations.

One of the more interesting such illustrations of the importance of sensory perception was the discovery several years ago that new mothers expected the food for their babies to taste especially good. While the manufacturers knew that young babies could not taste subtle variations in food flavors, passing the mother taste test was essential. To solve that problem, flavor additives were added to baby food products. Following a health scare, the practice was modified.

Psychological Factors Affecting Purchase Decisions. *Motivation* is perhaps the most basic psychological factor available to marketers. Most consumers have a latent and passive set of felt needs. When such needs move from passive to active, when the consumer is motivated to do something about a situation, the best marketing opportunities occur. The key marketing question is "What will motivate a customer to become eager to purchase my product?" One set of answers to this question was posed about fifty years ago by psychologist Abraham Maslow. He presented a classification or hierarchy of human needs which marketers have used as a benchmark for understanding motivation ever since.

What Maslow recognized was that individuals pass through a predictable set of needs requiring satisfaction, depending on the person's sense of his or her position in life. Maslow observed that such needs represent what might be considered steps toward ultimate fulfillment. He also noted that individuals become motivated to strive to satisfy each set or plateau of needs only after satisfying the set of needs preceding it. Therefore, if the marketer can determine where a consumer or group of consumers is on the hierarchy, the marketer can then understand which appeals will "target" and motivate them.

The five stages of the hierarchy of needs as described by Maslow are:

1. *Physiological needs:* hunger, thirst, warmth, shelter
2. *Safety needs:* security, protection, order, stability
3. *Belonging needs:* affection, belonging, friendship
4. *Esteem needs:* self-respect, prestige, achievement
5. *Self-actualization needs:* self-fulfillment[1]

In some parts of the world, including very low income areas of the United States, the most basic physiological and safety needs are not yet being met. Aiming for this group, marketers sell food on the basis of its being filling, inexpensive, and nourishing. In most parts of the United States, as well as in many parts of the rest of the world, most individuals have fulfilled the two "lower" plateaus of needs. In reaching those customers, marketers sell food on the basis of stimulating taste, unique packaging, or convenience. Further up the hierarchy, food is sold on the basis of status—imported mustard, for instance, which is sold in the delicatessen department of the supermarket rather than in the condiment department.

Maslow's hierarchy helps explain the jelly bean product shift. Jelly

1. Derived from A. H. Maslow, *Motivation and Personality* (New York: Harper & Row, 1954).

beans had been sold for a number of years in inexpensive packages, consisting of five or six flavors, primarily to lower- and middle-income markets. When it was learned that then President Ronald Reagan liked and ate the product, marketers saw their opportunity to move it from the low end of the candy shelf. The revised products, consisting of dozens of flavors, were sold in specialty stores at ten times the price of the earlier product. Concurrently, many marketers withdrew or limited the supply of the more basic product, resulting in a dramatic consumption shift without much of the costly increase of capacity necessary had they attempted to provide for both market segments simultaneously. In this manner, the industry hedged against a future return to earlier jelly bean purchasing practices when the eating habits of Ronald Reagan were no longer trend-setting.

Learning is the accumulation of experience that is stored in our memory for future use. Much of our learning occurs passively over time from observation as well as from listening to others. Many people, for instance, think of the name General Electric as being synonymous with light bulbs, Xerox with copying machines, and Campbell's with soups. This is an enviable position for the marketer of those products to be in.

A new product that is introduced in such a way that it is favorably noticed (or learned) by the consumer has a better chance for sales when the purchase need arises. Thus, many companies send free samples and discount coupons redeemable for a new product in order to not only get the product out but to assist the learning process. A product that has not tested well and that is rejected by those who try it will have a much more difficult time later on, even after the flaw has been corrected; negative learning will have occurred in the minds of that first set of customers. It is much harder to change a mind once it is made up than it is to provide a good first impression.

Marketers for the American auto industry today are facing the negative impression problem, for experience has convinced many consumers that foreign cars are built better, require fewer repairs, and cost less for value received. American car makers attempted to overcome that bias with advertising campaigns touting their quality before improving their production processes, further reinforcing the already existing negative bias.

Carrying this concept a little further, it is important that the marketer emphasize to the customer that the credit for success—cleaner shirts—be given to the appropriate detergent rather than to a new washing machine or some other cause. This approach, called *attribu-*

tion theory, is the major focus of ads comparing the favored product with less effective competitors, reminding all that it is the particular product that makes the difference every time.

Attitude is a predisposition, built up over time, to have a favorable or unfavorable conviction about a situation or product. It is a learned response. So long as the dairy industry could convince us that "real" butter was better, it had a distinct advantage in the marketplace. Once margarine ads began to focus on the product's lower cholesterol content and other advantages, customer preferences shifted away from butter, requiring the dairy industry to step up reinforcement advertising.

The same problem has arisen in the beef industry, where long-standing positive attitudes toward red meat have turned negative as a result of health considerations. The response, with some success, has been to portray beef as a key ingredient in returning to traditional, meaning older, values. This "real meat" campaign was set in motion to take advantage of a perceived shift in political values toward a more conservative focus.

Values and beliefs are learned attitudes and perceptions, reinforced by external pressures. In the state of Maine, for instance, many citizens place a high value on thriftiness, so advertising stresses durability and dependability more than it does in California, where change and newness are stronger values. Farmers consider themselves to be self-sufficient, so marketers stress do-it-yourself handyman products to them, while focusing on easy-to-use food mixes to reach young urban married couples, who value convenience highly.

Coke Introduces a New Product and Then Scrambles. A good illustration of how a major consumer products company stumbled and had to quickly adjust its product, its labeling, and its advertising strategy as a result of failing to consider the importance of consumer perceptions and attitudes can be seen from the "New Coke" product introduction.

After analyzing the results of secretly conducted comparison taste tests between Coca-Cola and Pepsi Cola, top management of the Atlanta based Coca-Cola Company decided to modify the flavor of its product. With much hoopla, it introduced New Coke. It seemed logical enough, for the tests confirmed a consumer preference for the Pepsi flavor. The preference was strongest with younger consumers, those most likely to buy the product over the long run. Pepsi had also been gaining on Coke for a number of years. What actually happened, however, was the creation of an enormous amount of consumer outrage toward the company and its products and a general boycott of New Coke.

What the company had unknowingly done was to tamper with a product that was generally viewed as a national institution, part of the good life in America, as reinforced by promotions stressing that Coke was "the real thing." And it did so with no warning and no adequate reasons provided. To make things worse, the change was carried out by a company that had spent years nurturing an image of wholesomeness and social responsibility and that had sponsored many noteworthy public service projects to reinforce that image.

Once the company realized the root of the problem, it took corrective action. The original product was reintroduced and was labeled "Coke Classic," a brand name that carried with it the recognition of the long heritage of the product's identity. That done, the company proceeded to introduce a number of variously flavored sugar and sugar-free products under the Coke name, including the new modified product flavor. The combined new products quickly calmed the outcry.

Had Coca-Cola's management taken the time to determine the consumer's emotional perception of the product by trying to gauge consumer reaction to having a different product in containers bearing the Coca-Cola label, it would have saved itself a great deal of trouble.

Interpersonal Influences. Each of us is influenced not only by our internal thoughts but by those around us—our families and reference groups. These are the people who most shape our experiences and learning and by whom we wish most to be respected.

Reference groups are those groups with which one has a continuing contact and relationship. Thus, families, close friends, employees in the same office, members of the country club, and members of a college fraternity play an important role in the study and use of consumer behavior. Since each of us seeks ideas and approval from others for purchasing decisions, these groups represent the natural major influences on such decisions. Let us look at several of these groups separately.

Families are small groups of related people who normally live together, continually interacting and modifying each other's behavior. A family consisting of parents—increasingly only one parent—and children is called a *nuclear family*. A family that includes grandparents and other relatives living nearby and spending time together is called an *extended family*. These groupings are important to marketers because there is a complex interplay among them that affects purchasing decisions. The decision of where to eat on a family outing, for instance, typically results from a broad discussion among all members.

The process of give-and-take in the discussion shifts, depending on the structural relationships within a family, as well as on the perceived degree of expertise of a particular family member. So close and so constantly do members of the family live and interact that often the original purchase decision is modified in order to take into account the concerns of other family members. Along the way, certain family members become the dominant influence in particular product category purchase decisions. Wives typically are dominant in the purchase of food, soft drinks, personal care products, furnishings, and kitchen appliances. Husbands are dominant in outdoor equipment, insurance, and entertainment units (VCRs, stereos, TVs). Children tend to be dominant in breakfast cereals, snacks, and cookies.

Consumer behavior analysis has shown that long-standing assumptions about family purchasing dominance can be wrong and that dramatic changes can result. Marketers believed that men made the family car purchase decisions, so showrooms were bright and barren and salesmen were trained to focus on the male shopper even when the wife was along. Now it is recognized that the wife plays the key final modifying decision role, accommodated by the husband. So showrooms are now carpeted, with background music, and salespeople treat women as important participants.

In items of communal family use, complex compromises can occur. Minivans have become popular primarily because they provide easier access and better riding conditions for the kids than station wagons, which were compromise purchase vehicles. Second and third TV sets are often purchased in order to enable each family segment to watch different shows at the same time. Marketers wishing to sell products for family use advertise product ideas that assist the primary purchasers in gaining general family acceptance for their purchase choice. For example, vacation site brochures must provide acceptable entertainment for all members of the family, including good restaurants, health clubs, game rooms, and shopping facilities. Shopping mall developers have found that food courts and theaters increase total family shopping, providing leisure activities for the husband and children while other family members shop.

Family life style is the tendency of a family, and other reference groups, to develop common sets of attitudes, expectations, and behavior over time. Many families go camping, eat out regularly, get interested in new clothes, spend most of their income, or become very reluctant to spend without reviewing their options very carefully. It has been found that when they leave the immediate family, individuals tend to retain most of its purchasing attitudes.

Family Life Cycles. A dependable predictor of certain types of purchasing behavior is the family life cycle, the various stages a family goes through over time as shown in Figure 5-1. A marketer can chart passages through a typical family life cycle and develop expectations of purchasing behavior based on each stage. As the family passes through each stage, different consumer priorities emerge and income shifts. Unmarried young and middle-aged people spend primarily for their own need-filling pleasure. When they marry, a shift to encompass the requirements of a new household occurs. Similarly, the presence of young children requires a further shift.

For marketers, the stage of the family life cycle is more important that the age at which an event occurs. The family that postpones having its first child in order for the wife to pursue a career demonstrates purchasing characteristics similar to those of a younger family with a child, although the older family may be able to afford more expensive items.

Admittedly simplified, Figure 5-1 is not inclusive; it does not identify young divorced with and without children, stages of the development of childhood, and other common variations. Such segments of an extended model are equally important to marketers as consumer behavior predictors.

Household is a term used to cover a person or group of persons living together. It represents the basic purchasing unit for heat, food, appliances, telephones, and many other items necessary for the operation of a housing unit. In that sense, the family represents a subset of the household. Two or more friends living together as roommates and strangers sharing adjoining rooms in a dwelling are also households, so long as there is some interchange and shared usage of products and facilities. Nonfamily households do not, however, have the same degree of reference-group relationship as do families.

Other reference groups, such as friends who spend a lot of time together, members of a tight-knit social organization, employees of a corporation, and active church members, become important influences in the decision-making process. Such groups, like families, help

Figure 5-1. Stages of a typical family life cycle.

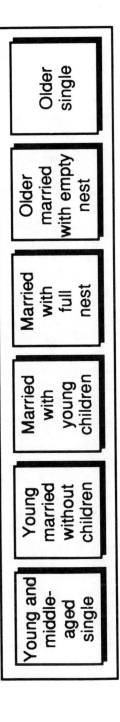

foster certain values and attitudes. Being stylish may become important to all members of a group, with each attempting to purchase and wear the trendiest clothing. Other groups, particularly those associated with a hobby, such as classic cars, ham radios, gardening, and travel, encourage their members to determine and purchase the latest, and frequently most expensive, equipment and supplies.

Most reference groups impact the behavior of their members. Notice the similarities in the appearance of executives going into a particular corporation, workers going into a plant entrance, students attending the same college, and families going on vacation. Teenage gangs in poor inner-city neighborhoods not only wear similar clothing as identifying uniforms but also purchase sneakers, frequently having fifty to one hundred or more pairs. These are typically neatly arranged by style, each in many colors and combinations of colors; many of them are very expensive. Marketers, recognizing the *norms*—the accepted behavior of such gangs—advertise their sneakers with promotions featuring black celebrities wearing their particular brand and enjoying themselves in spacious surroundings. The same marketers spend considerable amounts of money to have their sneakers worn in pop videos shown on MTV and other media watched by inner-city teens.

Still another important element of reference-group activity has to do with a person's *self-perception*—that is, how a person thinks of herself and how she wishes others to see her. In defining our self-perception, we look toward individuals we consider to be *opinion leaders*—those who are first in setting fashion or language tone. Others follow the lead of such people in dress, product choices, phrasing, and other cultural characteristics. Although each of us looks to someone as an opinion leader, we tend to choose different opinion leaders for different purposes. Thus, for purchasing a car we might look to a different opinion leader than for purchasing clothes. If a marketer can identify and obtain the support of an opinion leader, such as frequently occurs in the women's fashion clothing market, she can use these leaders to have an important impact on shifting fashion trends.

Encompassing Influences. In addition to those influences to which each of us responds internally and those provided by the people near us on a continuing basis, other powerful forces reinforce the culture and society we live in. Sociologists and anthropologists have shown us that these external influences, like the other two, are important to marketers trying to attract consumer attention.

Culture is the all-encompassing environment in which we live. It is the heritage of customs, beliefs, and attitudes presented to us as we move about within our society. It builds characteristics over time that set standards and margins for acceptable behavior. In the most sweeping sense, a knowledge of cultural values not only assists marketers in adapting their messages but is equally important in helping marketers avoid creating a conflict by espousing ideas contrary to the dominant culture. In the dominant U.S. culture, literacy is valued, so marketers can endorse education, sell encyclopedias, and project their products by having them identified with people who are articulate and educated. In the Amish-American and Mexican-American cultures, however, children tend to leave school early to help support the rest of the family; in these markets, literacy, high school education, and college attendance are controversial issues which marketers may find it best to avoid.

Both U.S. and European cultures encourage changing styles in women's clothing, so advertising new fashions is quite common in those cultures. In Moslem cultures, clothing styles for women do not change quickly, so producers of such products should seek markets elsewhere.

The records are full of marketers who attempted, to their sorrow, to take their successful marketing approach from one culture to another without paying attention to cultural differences. The first McDonald's restaurants in Paris failed miserably, for the French had little respect for either fast food or hamburgers. The French culture places a high value on the time needed for good food preparation, and sandwiches are not a dominant product. The entrepreneur who established a brewery in Egypt failed to appreciate that Moslems don't drink alcohol. In this case, however, the desperate owner eventually recognized that the ingredients of beer—malt, wheat, and hops—have strong nutritional values. He succeeded by boiling off the alcohol and selling his new nonalcoholic health drink.

Cultures change over time. The U.S. culture, for instance, has become more diet- and health-conscious during the last twenty years, with hard liquor giving way to wine and fast food to health food; the use of cigarettes has shifted from being socially acceptable to becoming socially objectionable.

Influences of Subcultures. Every general culture gets broken down into *subcultures,* groupings that, while following the general lead of the enveloping general culture, have differing characteristics in some ways. Thus, ethnic groups, racial backgrounds, religious heritage, and regional locations all represent examples of subcultures. These subcultures represent targeting opportunities for marketers, and many companies market products aimed especially at ethnic groups. Goya products dominate the Hispanic food market in the eastern United States; in the same way, Progresso and Rokeach dominate the ethnic Italian and Jewish food markets, respectively. Certain other products are sold across several markets with differing advertising and separate labeling but with the same content. For example, in recent years Mexican-style food products have begun to be marketed to broader markets, with more descriptive labeling in the new markets to assist customers in understanding how such products should be used for best results.

The increasing availability of media directed at specific ethnic groups has assisted subculture marketers greatly. Many newspapers and magazines are written for such groups; radio and television stations aimed exclusively at black, Hispanic, Chinese, German, and other ethnic groupings abound. The Time Warner cable franchises in the boroughs of Brooklyn and Queens in New York City offer programming in ten languages, including Hebrew and Hindi, on their seventy-five channels and are planning to offer more. The fastest-growing media exist in the Hispanic community, with two full-fledged national television networks flourishing.

A case in point is the TV program *Sabado Gigante*. A three-hour variety show produced in Miami, it consistently has among the highest ratings in most major markets across the United States. Although it charges some of the highest advertising rates, marketers hawking products from cosmetics to cars, from refreshments to clothing, scramble to get a chance to be on the program. And yet the average person does not know that it even exists.

Sabado Gigante, or "Big Saturday," is a prime-time Saturday evening Spanish-language variety show. It has a dynamic host, a regular cast, guest artists, audience participation activities, special sections on issues of the day, and telephone contests. The advertisers read like a Who's Who of consumer products: Coca-Cola, Hershey's Chocolate, McDonald's, Toyota, Purina Puppy Chow. Many of the ads are prepared especially for the program and represent as much as anything the maturing of the Spanish-speaking TV networks and the size of the broad Hispanic middle-class market. One of the major appeals of advertising on this particular program is the opportunity it provides marketers to present their products to the audience as "theirs," in language, dress, and environment—to place them inside the subculture.

Marketers are beginning to recognize that our cultural background can affect the way we do things and the way we respond to messages. Cultural anthropologists for Xerox are studying worker behavior in stress and nonstress situations in order to make products more "user friendly," to improve training programs for users of new equipment, and to upgrade its repair team training. They have, for instance, developed software programs with several choices, depending on the employee's cultural background, thus providing more options for strong performance than had previously been the case.

Each of us, as we move through changing situations, continues to seek information on what is considered good taste in our particular environment. In certain companies, such as IBM, in which a distinctive style of dress is favored, the task of *acculturation*, or fitting in, is easy. In other companies, the learning takes on many more diverse forms. As shifts occur in subcultures—as women, blacks, and Hispanics move into managerial ranks, for example—marketers spend much of their advertising providing information on appropriate clothing for certain situations. Such ads are good examples of the learning process in action.

Some subcultures hold values that conflict with those of other subcultures, and these clashes represent a potential risk for marketers in certain circumstances. Advertising female personal hygiene products through the general media poses a problem for pharmaceutical marketers such as Johnson & Johnson, since those viewers who believe that such products should not be advertised to family audiences may respond by deciding not to purchase other items in J&J's product line.

In other cases, some subcultures have product needs that are almost directly opposite those of other subcultures. Thus, ads for hair relaxers are typically promoted in media aimed predominantly at black women, while hair curling products are advertised in media primarily used by white women.

Social class is the grouping of society into categories based on certain characteristics, including beliefs, attitudes, life styles, influence, wealth, education, and position within a community. Each of us has elements of several social class strata. A working mother may be the daughter of the mayor of a high-income community and the cousin of the president of a large bank. Over time, however, one of the elements of status tends to dominate, and we are viewed and perceive ourselves as fitting within a particular class.

In the United States, the most common delineation of social class groupings is:

Upper class: Corporate and military elite; people with high levels of influence and with prestigious connections; university-educated persons with income derived from varied sources

Upper middle class: Professionals and upper-level executives; successful owners of dominant small businesses; college-educated persons with well-above-average incomes

Middle class: Middle-level managers; semiprofessionals; persons with high school attendance and some college education; people with above-national-average incomes

Working class: Low-paid skilled and service workers; frequent job changers; those with some high school; people with living standards below the national average

Underclass: A category of people characterized by high unemployment, high illiteracy, welfare dependency, and a living standard below poverty level

From a marketing standpoint, a social class consists of groupings whose general perspectives and purchasing behaviors are similar, providing purchasing predictability. Upper-class individuals tend to read *Archeology Magazine, The New Yorker, Forbes,* and the *New York Times.* They shop in specialty stores and attend the symphony. Working-class members tend to watch situation dramas on TV, shop at K mart, attend professional wrestling matches, and read a tabloid.

Each group seeks different qualities in the products they buy. Price is not the only attribute distinguishing products bought by members of different social classes. For example, a much higher proportion of upper-middle- and upper-class consumers buy imported cars than is true of working-class consumers. This applies even to the less costly and fuel-efficient smaller foreign cars. Working-class purchasers in the United States continue to have an aversion to foreign-made autos and other products made overseas.

Automakers take advantage of this phenomenon. Makers of inexpensive foreign cars stress middle- and upper-class values in their advertising, showing scenes of neatly dressed drivers in pleasant surroundings, whereas U.S. automakers stress patriotism and traditional values in their low-cost-car promotions.

In the U.S. market, the middle classes are so large that they afford very attractive broad-based marketing opportunities. Significant numbers of marketing appeals are focused on that especially large market segment. In many other countries, however, social class structure is more rigid, with lines more clearly drawn. In such environments, specific class pride is stronger than it is in the United States. This reality provides broad access to marketing opportunities. In England, for instance, alcohol advertisements for different brands stress specific social class use as a major theme in their presentations.

The smaller social class reference group on which a person bases his or her purchasing behavior is called a *life style* group. This smaller social class grouping is particularly useful to marketers, for it reflects especially closely related behavior. Young urban professionals tend to purchase the same brands of clothing, the same foods, the same kinds of cars; rural blue-collar workers tend to enjoy the same entertainment, purchase the same brands of beer, have a high level of patriotism, and resent change. Each group has its own generally recognized norms and values, which each associating member tends to follow. A life style relationship is considered by marketers to be one of the strongest estimators of purchasing behavior, considerably more important than income.

ORGANIZATIONAL BUYING BEHAVIOR

In this chapter we have so far focused on the purchasing behavior of consumers. Now we focus on the buying behavior of organizations, why it differs from what has already been presented, and how that difference affects the marketer's role. What follows should be more familiar ground for most readers, for it relates more directly to the work situation. It may also explain why certain purchasing outcomes are not what was originally expected. But first, a definition.

Definition of Organizational Buying Behavior

Organizational buying behavior encompasses those activities corporations and governments go through in making purchasing decisions and the influences, pressures, and considerations involved in the process. The term "purchasing" is not limited to physical possession of a product but includes services, warranties, recognition of ideas, and related considerations. While this definition is similar to that presented for consumer behavior, the differences in actual purchasing behavior and the impact of those decisions are dramatic.

The Nature of the Organizational Market

Whereas the consumer market is characterized by many potential customers, the organizational market is characterized by the existence of only a small number of potential customers. The consumer market is spread broadly geographically; the organizational market tends to be concentrated in clusters. While consumers purchase frequently and in small quantities, organizations purchase less frequently and in large quantities. Finally, while the consumer purchases products for the satisfaction derived from their use, organizations purchase products in order either to place them as parts in their own final product or to use them in the course of their operations. For example:

- USX purchases coal and iron ore, highly concentrated oxygen, and rolling and stamping machinery, among other materials, to produce steel.

- Dodge Division purchases rolled steel, seat covers and seat belts, spark plugs and distributors, windshields and wipers, radios, and speedometers, among other items, to be placed in new cars and trucks on the assembly line.

- Tandy purchases disk drives, memory chips, modems, keyboards, and monitors, among other parts, to place in the personal computers bearing the Radio Shack brand name.

- Burger King purchases raw and processed food products, paper and plastic cartons and containers, stoves, and liquid dispensing equipment, among other items, to operate its business.

- The Red Cross purchases refrigerators and warmers, bandages and medical supplies, ambulances and trucks, and other products to operate its services.

- The U.S. Department of Education purchases or leases computers and printers, telephones and copying machines, desks and file cabinets, postage meters and sorters, and other items to perform its designated responsibility.

- In addition, all of these organizations purchase a plethora of utilities, supplies, and services necessary for them to operate.

Other characteristics of organizational buying can be noted. The organizational market has a "derived" rather than a direct demand; its need for most products is dependent on the potential sales of its products and services, not on the purchaser's own satisfaction in use. In addition, organizational demand is "inelastic"; price is not the most important consideration. When the demand for their product is strong, companies will pay what they must in order to purchase the products and services they need to operate. Conversely, a lowered price will attract little attention from companies during periods in which their own products and services are not selling.

The Behavior of Organizational Markets

We have already noted the complexity of the behaviors involved in consumer purchasing and the varied influences and considerations that go into consumers' final decisions. The organizational market is equally complex, but for different reasons. These influences include:

- *Use of full-time purchasers*. Organizational purchasers tend to be professional, spending most or all of their time in the purchasing function. They also tend to be technically knowledgeable.
- *Dominance of rational behavior*. Since organizational customers are making their purchases for the benefit of the company as opposed to purchasing for their own use, a key consideration is the degree to which a particular product fits the specifications necessary for its use. Thus, purchasers must look for durability, completeness of specifications, reliability of quality, dependability of supply and of support services, promptness of delivery, terms of purchase, ability to return excess supply, and price.
- *Impact of reciprocal purchasing*. It is only natural that a company give special consideration in purchasing products it needs to a company that purchases its products, to the benefit of both. This is commonly known as reciprocal behavior.
- *Political/policy considerations*. Many organizations have policies encouraging the purchase of products under special conditions. Such policies include buying some products from minority-owned companies, buying some products in the local community when possible, buying from suppliers in locations that the company considers to be growing markets for its products, and buying from companies whose marketers have demonstrated an appreciation for the business obtained.
- *Desire to maintain strong producer/supplier relationships*. Many companies place orders for products with strong, loyal suppliers in order

to stabilize their sources of materials. These arrangements make the supplier in essence an element in the production line of the purchaser. Such arrangements are increasing as more companies reduce their warehousing functions and contract for delivery of products "JIT" (just in time) to meet assembly timetables.

▪ *Significance of face-to-face contact.* Because of technical considerations, the complexity of the transactions, and the importance of each order, there is considerable personal contact between organizational buyers and marketers.

▪ *Flexible, negotiated pricing.* Because quantities may vary and quality elements can be modified under certain considerations, pricing is often negotiated as part of the marketing process and can vary from organization to organization.

▪ *Choice between leasing and purchasing.* In some instances, when purchasers appear to be losing interest or find they do not have the money to spend at a given time, they opt for leasing arrangements, which may lead to future purchases.

Purchasers also give consideration to the desires of senior executives who have come across a product advertisement or who have had a discussion on a product with other executives and wish to try it out.

The Organizational Purchasing Decision Process

The stages of the organizational purchasing decision process are identical to those noted at the beginning of this chapter at the discussion of the consumer purchasing decision process: recognizing a problem, searching for information, assessing the alternatives, making a purchase decision, and conducting postpurchase evaluations. But the conduct of the process is not at all similar. The number of people involved, the thoroughness of the assessment of the situation, the nature of the technical comparison of alternatives, and the impact of the final decision are each dramatically different.

The Buying Center. Many people are involved in the purchasing process in most organizations. Marketing theorists have coined the label "buying center" to encompass all the people and activities involved in a purchasing decision, and thus all the people of whom the marketer must be aware. If the buying center consists of a formal committee, its membership can be quite readily approached. When, as frequently is the case, a more informal and changing group make up the buying center, the marketer's task is more complex.

Members of the Buying Center. A buying center normally has a purchasing agent or other purchasing personnel at its heart. There is typically also an engineer or other technical personnel involved, as well as people from the departments seeking the product under study. There are also the influencers—the company's own marketers who may wish the purchase to go to a company with which they are doing business or with which they wish to do business.

Another source of pressure on the company's marketers may derive from the impact that the purchase of a particular product might have on the balance of competition within the company. Pressure may come from another department that may have a secondary use for the product, or it may come from a department that wishes costs to remain low or the purchase not to be made at all. There may also be pressures from other levels of management, depending on particular circumstances.

Implications for Marketers. To influence this complex process, a marketer must stay involved, continue to search out concerns, demonstrate how the product or service under consideration will solve them, and be fully aware of both the strengths and the weaknesses of his or her own product within the competition taking place.

The alert marketer attempts to sort out the people in the buying center by finding answers to such questions as, What are the roles being played by the members of the buying center? What are the objectives of those participating in the process? What are the appeals that will assist in winning over each member of the team? It is also important to learn who is serving as "gatekeeper"—the person (typically a purchasing agent) responsible for asking questions, obtaining answers for the group, and passing that information along. The marketer also tries to learn how accurately the information is being passed along.

Bypassing the gatekeeper in order to provide support for a company's products results in marketers advertising so broadly in business and government magazines and journals, providing so many displays at trade shows, having so many business luncheons, and corresponding so broadly within a company once a buying center has been identified that the marketing function becomes much more expensive.

At this point it is important to remember that most companies do not designate a group of people as a formal purchasing committee or buying center. Rather, the buying center is a framework marketers use to understand the various roles and the behavior that occurs during the organizational purchasing process.

Government Purchasing Behavior

While much of the purchasing by local, state, and federal governments follows the procedures described for other organizations, several special characteristics of the process result in altered purchasing behavior that deserves special note.

To begin with, the size of the government market is massive, as is the diversity of products purchased. It has been said, perhaps not in jest, that anything sold elsewhere is also purchased by government procurement people somewhere. The government purchasing process developed over time, with the special attention given it by various public officials, legislatures, courts, and the general public, has resulted in a far more formal and complex system.

Purchasing is performed in the open, with quantities of key information available about the process, the specifications sought, previous prices quoted, and the actual products purchased and vendors used. The purchase agreements received by a successful marketer are also made public. This openness results in significantly more paperwork and very detailed written negotiations. Other important elements of the process are:

- *Published purchasing procedures.* Government agencies publish detailed procedures, including forms to be issued, applicable bidding dates, dates by which the agency will make its decision, and the process for appeals of rejected bids.

- *"RFP" bidding process.* Most government procurement is done through a form known as an RFP (request for purchase), released by a government agency with specifications included. Marketers, after obtaining all the information they can, then submit their bids in writing.

- *Low-bid stipulation.* Under requirements sometimes made explicit but always important even when not stated, price is a key consideration. Price in this case is not limited to a single figure but includes services offered, reliability, and past performance. All other things being equal, the lowest-priced bid receives the order.

- *Approved on list.* In a number of product categories, once some of a company's products have been accepted by the agency, additional purchases of other products can be made. Thus, obtaining approved-vendor status is a key element in doing large amounts of business with a government agency.

  ■ *Restrictive conduct-of-business rules.* The last key element of the government purchasing relationship is the restrictions imposed on marketers. Frequently, no lunches can be purchased for government employees; samples and gifts cannot be given to prospective purchasers. Contracts combining reciprocity and future relationships cannot be used in making the sale.

Other Organizational Customers

While our presentation has focused on manufacturing and governmental organizations, the principles apply to others. It makes no difference whether a company is operated in order to make a profit, whether it is publicly or privately owned, or whether the marketer is a vendor or a producer. What does matter is the intent of the purchaser and the role of the marketing effort in successfully meeting that end.

  We hope this chapter has given readers a stronger appreciation for why marketers spend so much of their time on these behavioral areas, which are so imprecise and yet very valuable to the marketing task. The value of the material covered can be put to the test easily; readers need only pay attention to their own purchasing behavior as consumers, and as company representatives.

PART THREE

Structuring the Strategic Marketing Plan

CHAPTER 6

Planning and Its Impact on a Market-Driven Organization

A company's plan is a document linking the functions of the organization—any size organization. These functions include product development, production, service, and finance, as well as distribution, marketing, sales, and any other operational areas. Planning is the mental process that creates a company's vision of a marketplace and decides what the business can and should be. It then shapes that vision into products and services and uses strategies and tactics to package, market, and support them. Planning also permits managers to assess the competitive environment, anticipate competitive trends, and take proactive initiatives. Through these actions, a business achieves advantage and delivers customer satisfaction.

In this chapter we discuss the job of planning. We explore the benefits of planning, look at the use of multifunctional management teams in an organized planning process, and present an outline of a long-term strategic marketing plan.

THE JOB OF PLANNING

The primary goal of planning in a market-driven organization is to provide a definable, repeatable, and predictable process that specifies how to accomplish the following steps:

111

Step 1: *Understand Markets and Select Opportunities*

Having once sought macro (mass) markets, Procter & Gamble (P&G) executives now seek opportunities by looking at micro (focused) markets (also known as market niches, segments, or targets). Markets are examined on factors such as age, income, family status, occupation, education, religion/race/nationality, social class, life style, and buying behavior patterns.

P&G moved a dozen executives (including both marketing and nonmarketing members of a multifunctional management team) to the offices of one of its most important customers, Wal-Mart Stores, Inc., to shape a joint plan with its managers. The planning effort resulted in the following actions:

1. Specific market segments were prioritized within major Wal-Mart locations.
2. Market research studies were initiated to gather data about current users, competitor's users, and nonusers of various products.
3. Promotional campaigns were tailored to those market segments representing greatest potential.
4. Physical distribution was updated using satellite communications from Wal-Mart locations to P&G, which provided daily sales data so that orders could be shipped automatically, resulting in just-in-time (JIT) delivery with near-perfect results—a remarkable 99.6 percent on-time delivery.

Step 2: *Define Customer Requirements and Identify Solutions*

Black & Decker, which manufactures products for the home, garden, and industrial markets, moved from a floundering market position in the early 1980s to become a formidable worldwide competitor against aggressive Japanese and German rivals by the late 1980s. B&D managers—marketing and nonmarketing managers alike—worked, studied, talked, and sensitized themselves to customers' requirements. The managers then responded by strengthening product lines, pushing ahead with product innovations, and bolstering distribution systems to assist customers in solving their competitive problems.

For example, catering to the do-it-yourself home segment, B&D focused on using channels of distribution to create cost efficiencies for retail accounts. B&D combined shipments of complementary products for do-it-your-selfers with such items as door locks and decorative faucets, along with its primary product line of power tools, to help retailers increase store sales volume.

Then, to assist its customers in maintaining a competitive edge, a powerhouse of new products was developed, including space-saving coffee makers with thermal carafes, toasters with wider slots, upscale food choppers, and cordless power wrenches and screwdrivers. B&D introduced drill bits that last seven times longer than previous ones and industrial tools with new, longer-lasting battery packs.

Step 3: Coordinate Activities Across Several Operating Units to Produce (or Obtain) Products and Services and Integrate Them Into Total Solutions

Mitsubishi Electric is an example of how a company with a high-technology, production-driven orientation coordinated the talents of marketing and nonmarketing groups and applied classic marketing technique. Four steps demonstrate the technique:

1. *Tune into market problems and provide product solutions.* During the late 1970s, both technical and marketing people at Mitsubishi observed that large-screen TV pictures were blurry, with distracting and annoying hues of blues, greens, and reds. They determined to focus on solving this important problem. Result: Today, over 300,000 Americans own 35-inch TVs with the Mitsubishi nameplate or a Mitsubishi-made picture tube. As of 1990, there was virtually no competition in the high-end niche for 35-inch sets selling at $2,400 and up; worldwide, the company grabbed 40 percent of the fastest-growing segment of the TV market.

2. *Differentiate, innovate—don't imitate.* As one Mitsubishi executive states, "If we only imitate others, we can't produce good profits. We need to be first." But innovation should complement the basic strengths of a company. For example, Mitsubishi already owned video technology from its experience in radarscopes and video displays for aerospace and defense applications. Product developers applied their technical know-how to introduce push-button electronic tuning, reduce reflected lights, and improve color purity.

3. *Locate a niche that is emerging, neglected, or poorly served.* Market sensitivity is an acquired cultural characteristic. Mitsubishi managers from many functional areas displayed such sensitivity when, after

much joint effort, they identified a market niche for projection TVs. Applying product solutions to market opportunities resulted in a 45-inch TV with projection behind the screen instead of in front, all contained in a cabinet not much deeper than that of a conventional TV. What followed was a continuing rollout of products: from 50-inch-projection to 120-inch-projection TVs.

4. *Use marketing innovations.* The components of the marketing mix are product, price, promotion, and distribution. Each of the components represents a major function of the organization. In turn, the managers from those functions have input into the planning activities.

Here's how the mix worked for Mitsubishi. First, managers positioned their product innovation as a unique, differentiated product, which in turn supported premium pricing. Promotion zeroed in on the product claim that the large screen is a "home theater." Then the company employed an innovative distribution strategy. Instead of using mass market distribution and going head-to-head against Sony with its 45,000 retail outlets, it focused on exclusive distribution through a small, highly motivated dealer network with about 3,300 storefronts. Both dealers and Mitsubishi prospered while maintaining the high-quality, exclusive image.

To follow through on the exclusivity strategy, Mitsubishi used an additional merchandising device by introducing the Three Diamond credit card. It offered approved first-time buyers a $5,000 credit line. The tactic aimed at preventing customers from putting the purchase on another credit card. Buyers who used the cards became a somewhat captive audience for repeat purchases and exclusive offers for other equipment.

Step 4: Deliver and Support Solutions Consistent With Organizational and Market Requirements

Motorola, using the planning process as the unifying effort to meet its organizational and market requirements, mobilized to fight back and recapture its market position after near-devastating attacks from aggressive competitors during the mid-1980s. The remaking of Motorola focused on five primary categories, each of which is part of the planning process discussed later in this chapter.

First, Motorola changed its *company culture* from one of defeat to one of determination to survive and win. All managers were involved in determining that they could and would succeed—but only if they worked across functional areas to identify, create, and achieve their objectives. Motorola's new culture, an ingredient in determining strategic direction, is summarized by CEO George Fisher: "We intend to be the best manufacturer of electronics hardware in the world. There will be no more retreating or surrendering of markets."

Second, Motorola created a strategic *alliance* (a compact providing for cooperative use of contacts, expertise, and resources beneficial to both parties) with Toshiba. This relationship permitted Motorola to enter Japanese markets, where its sales skyrocketed by 70 percent in 1989. Additional strategic alliances are in effect worldwide as well as in the United States. Motorola has, for example, an agreement with IBM to develop breakthrough chip-making methods.

Third, Motorola stressed *product development*. Motorola reigned supreme in 1989 with two product innovations that sent its competitors clamoring to catch up. First, it developed the MicroTac cellular phone that slips into a coat pocket and flips open for use. Then came the first wristwatch pager, an ultrasmall product which looks like the Dick Tracy wrist radio. Both products are wonders in miniaturization.

Fourth, Motorola emphasized *quality*. Defects have been cut from nearly 3,000 per million products in 1983 to less than 200. The goal is to reach what is considered near-perfect manufacturing—3.4 defects per million products.

The highest acclaim for its quality efforts came in 1988, when Motorola won the esteemed Malcolm Baldrige National Quality Award. In 1989 the company was honored with Japan's Nikkei award for creative excellence in products and services.

Fifth, the company set up *organizational teams*. The traditional organizational hierarchy crumbled at Motorola. Design, manufacturing, and marketing people participate in teams to deliver cost-effective products that customers want. The results were amazing! For example, two-way radios were shipped in three days from receipt of order compared to thirty days just eighteen months before. New models of cellular phones began production just six months after the start of design compared to a lag of three years in 1985.

The four planning steps we have discussed demonstrate the diversity of activities that are part of the planning process, as seen in the context of the function of marketing management. Marketing management, you will recall from Chapter 1, is defined as a total system of interacting business activities designed to plan, price, promote, and distribute want-satisfying products and services to household and organizational users at a profit in a competitive environment.

BENEFITS OF PLANNING

How well an organization uses its resources—money, manpower, and materials—to create a competitive advantage determines the profitability of any market-driven operation. Planning makes the difference. Only a good planning system can take into account the exact amount of resources available, the exact state of the market, and probable trends in consumer wants and needs, and only after arriving at a plan can the manager manipulate the resources so that the company's offerings meet market conditions, satisfy the customer, and produce a profit.

If executed with skill by marketing and nonmarketing managers, a market-driven plan should result in the following benefits: organizing and facilitating clear thinking, emphasizing contingency plans of action, coordinating and unifying efforts, facilitating controls, and reducing risk.

Organizing and Facilitating Clear Thinking

Working out a plan instead of simply reacting to changes when they occur encourages managers to think efficiently. The process permits them to consider the facets and opportunities of a problem, to work out objectives and strategies for solving it, and to explain the course of action selected.

The planning process not only enables managers to check the logic behind each move but creates formats—give-and-take planning sessions with other managers or evaluation at other management levels—for evaluating the reasoning that goes into the plans of other managers. This process generally reveals a continuity of thinking among managers. While managers have their own way of handling or exploiting problems and opportunities, they should have the company's goal in mind. The process of organizing ideas, approaches, and alternatives develops clear thinking and improves the probability of reaching excellent decisions.

Emphasizing Contingency Plans of Action

The more thorough the planning, the more opportunity management has to consider and establish alternative courses of action. A manager can never be absolutely sure of how others will react to a move in the marketplace. By identifying planned alternatives, one for each possible reaction that may occur, the company prepares to keep pushing its marketing effort toward the goal, no matter what obstacles arise.

Motorola executives considered numerous contingencies, ranging from the radical move of selling its core business in microchips to Toshiba, thereby exiting the market, to the alternative it finally selected—deciding to remain in its position and fight. The driving force behind the choice stemmed from confidence in Motorola's native strengths in innovative product development and in its ability to regain world leadership in electronic products.

Coordinating and Unifying Efforts

Planning ensures that major undertakings receive all the attention they need, so that every move is coordinated. The introduction of a new product is a complicated job. Developers need to generate, examine, and get a product idea accepted; purchasers need to locate raw materials and organize a steady flow so that the materials are available as needed; manufacturing personnel have to establish a production schedule; financial people must create the budgeting and reporting system; and, finally, marketers must determine target markets, sales managers must organize the distribution network, and promotions people must develop a campaign.

Facilitating Controls

A careful plan is the only way a company can establish and maintain a system of good audits and controls so that management can monitor each activity within the company. First, management charts the company's direction and sets goals and deadlines for achieving them. Next, management sets up a communication system that periodically collects data on actual results compared to planned results and provides feedback for each time interval. This system keeps management's finger on the pulse of actual achievement and enables it to take necessary corrective action if the audits and controls show that the results of one activity are drastically out of line with projections.

Reducing Risk

Time is a simple but crucial factor in risk reduction. The chances of successful planning increase if managers have enough time to systematically project a vision for their company or product line and then create meaningful objectives and strategies. Similarly, risk is reduced if managers have the time to determine, based on objectives to be achieved, which marketing battles to fight and which to avoid. When managers take time to analyze their company's vision and action, they can make choices that avoid meaningless expenditures of money, material, and manpower resources that lead to no competitive advantage.

While managers need enough time to collect and analyze the necessary information that accurate planning provides, they also need to move as quickly as circumstances allow, to give themselves a better chance of gaining or maintaining a competitive advantage.

To underline the importance of planning, consider the following risks that a company faces without a good planning system:

- *Too much reliance on luck.* A company that does not plan may find itself particularly dependent on the whims of fortune. If fortune is favorable, perhaps the company will thrive—for a while. If fortune is unfavorable—and luck has a habit of changing—the company will suffer.

- *Increased probability of mistakes.* Improper planning or no planning at all increases the likelihood that the company will make a serious mistake, one that may cut deeply into profits and deprive the company of resources to explore new market and product development.

- *Poor morale and inefficiency.* A company that doesn't organize its planning has no guidelines for top executives to use to distinguish between the effective manager and the inefficient manager. This makes for low morale among those managers the company needs the most. The turnover of good personnel will be high as those who know they can do a good job leave to seek more recognition elsewhere, and the company will face the problem of replacing them.

- *Narrowing of range of maneuverability.* Without planning, too often a company overcommits its resources, leaving too little in reserve. Such a company may find itself in a poor position to move rapidly in case of an unexpected competitive action, especially in the intensely competitive 1990s. This point alone should be enough to encourage proper planning, for few things are remembered longer than a profitable opportunity lost to lack of maneuverability.

- *Possible bankruptcy and liquidation.* The company may not be able to pay its debts because it has overextended itself.

MULTIFUNCTIONAL MANAGEMENT TEAMS

In the three case examples cited in this chapter, there is one common organizational factor: success resulted from the actions of multifunctional (mostly nonmarketing) managers working on teams. As a result of the need to cut costs and the move toward empowering lower-level employees with greater authority and responsibility, traditional organizational hierarchies have crumbled, to be replaced by teams performing the activities of different functions. Companies form the teams in order to achieve a customer-driven organization that is responsive to regionalized markets, attentive to customer needs, and positioned favorably to achieve a competitive advantage.

Multifunctional teams are also known as business management teams (BMTs) or product management teams (PMTs), depending on their level in the organization and their focus. The BMT takes responsibility for a broad look at an industry or a market, while the PMT focuses on a product or product line and usually comprises staff at a lower organizational level than that of the BMT. (To simplify the following explanation of team responsibilities, the single designation of BMT will stand for both BMT and PMT.)

BMTs simplify the system of control and shorten the chain of command. They put the company in a more flexible, maneuverable position by opening lines of communication between organizational functions that contribute to market success. In conventional organizational structures, every extra link in the chain means lost time in getting vital information to and from the head office; each unnecessary link weakens management's grasp of the situation, because it becomes more remote from the situation. The system of BMTs, in contrast, streamlines a company's internal communication, heightening efficiency.

With the rapid movement of information, managers must expect the unexpected and be able to adapt quickly and effectively. Companies organized into BMTs are in a better position to take advantage of fast-breaking local market opportunities and to respond with flexibility.

Duties and Responsibilities of a Business Management Team

The BMT serves as a significant functional contributor to the strategic marketing planning process, with leadership roles in:

1. Analyzing the environmental, industry, competitor, and customer situations
2. Defining the business or product-line strategic direction
3. Developing long- and short-term objectives
4. Formulating market, product, price, promotion, and distribution strategies to achieve objectives

Specific duties and responsibilities of a BMT include:

1. Recommending new products
2. Approving all major product/service alterations or modifications
3. Developing formal communications channels for field product needs
4. Planning and implementing strategies throughout the product life cycle
5. Developing programs to improve market position and profitability
6. Identifying market and product opportunities based on changing buying patterns
7. Coordinating efforts with various functions to achieve long- and short-term objectives
8. Coordinating efforts for interdivisional exchanges of new market or product opportunities (if possible)
9. Developing a team-generated strategic marketing plan

A BMT IN ACTION

An actual situation at Dow Chemical Company illustrates a BMT in action (some details in the following incident are disguised). An Indianapolis-based Dow salesperson of plastic resins identified a shift in strategy implemented by two competitors, leading manufacturers of similar plastic resins. The competitors suddenly moved away from the traditional channel of distribution, which linked producer to distributors to dealers to end users. Instead, the competitors bypassed distributors and sold directly to dealers and end users, potentially cutting their costs and perhaps providing quicker service. The salesperson recognized that this fast-moving change in strategy could create a problem for Dow—or, perhaps, an opportunity.

Telephoning that market intelligence in to Dow headquarters in

Midland, Michigan, led to a rapid response from a hastily called meeting of the BMT working with that product line. Following a thorough discussion of the situation, the BMT recommended strategies to its team leader. The team leader, a product manager, called eighteen of Dow's top distributors into a meeting at Chicago's O'Hare Airport within forty-eight hours of the phone call. The distributors were primed through a short workshop developed and presented by the Dow BMT on how to develop competitive marketing strategies.

They then entered group discussion sessions to recommend what strategies and tactics Dow could execute to counter the competitive threat from the two companies. The result was a series of recommendations—from those distributors who were bypassed—that created opportunities for Dow. The rapid response from the BMT solidified the relationships of Dow with the distributors, at the expense of the competitors, and Dow gained immediate support from distributors in implementing the plans, as well as a preferred customer status with those distributors for its approach and loyalty. Only through the quick reaction of a BMT empowered to take action could the competitive action have been turned into an opportunity.

THE STRATEGIC MARKETING PLAN

We now consider the organization of the Strategic Marketing Plan. The plan is divided into two parts. The first, which defines the long-term strategic view of a business, division, or product line, is presented here; the second, the short-term tactical marketing plan, is presented in Chapter 7.

Figure 6-1 consists of four sections in the long-term strategic marketing plan: strategic direction, objectives and goals, growth strategies, and business portfolio.

Strategic Direction

The strategic direction, also known as the mission, permits the manager and the planning group to consider the long-range philosophy of a business unit. It is a strategic vision of what the team can and should be.

Figure 6-1. Long-term strategic marketing plan (3–5 years).

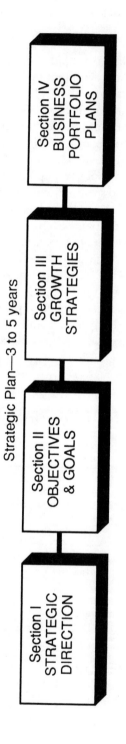

Strategic Plan—3 to 5 years

Section I
STRATEGIC
DIRECTION

Section II
OBJECTIVES
& GOALS

Section III
GROWTH
STRATEGIES

Section IV
BUSINESS
PORTFOLIO
PLANS

Developing strategic direction requires thoughtful consideration of the following questions:

1. *What are our distinctive areas of expertise?* Determine by analyzing strengths and weaknesses which distinctive competencies exist, as related to customer needs and compared with competition. Look at product development, production capability, and service follow-through, as well as distribution facilities, selling efficiencies, and the special skills of individuals.

2. *What business should we be in, looking ahead three to five years?* Ask if the nature of the business will be the same or if it will be necessary to change the direction of activities performed or products delivered.

3. *What customers should we serve?* Will you serve intermediaries such as jobbers and distributors, or will you reach out to end users?

4. *Which customer functions should we satisfy?* Customers' problems become your problems if you want to retain their business. That axiom stands at the center of a customer-driven orientation. Try to forecast the type of service, delivery, product quality, and technical assistance required to provide solutions to customers' problems.

5. *What ways (technologies) should we use to satisfy future customer/ market needs?* Electronic data interchange (EDI), computer-aided design (CAD), and computer-aided manufacturing (CAM) are examples of technologies available to create competitive advantage. Determine what your company will need.

Be aware of changes taking place in the markets, in consumer behavior, and in the competitive, environmental, cultural, and/or economic climate. Consider the total external environment; business is no longer localized, even though your business may be confined to a specific geographic area. Economic swings prevail, affecting local as well as world economies, labor costs, and global competition. These factors, in turn, influence your company's strategic direction.

A strategic marketing plan permits you to contemplate your business from both a narrow and a wide perspective and to make appropriate choices. For example, study the narrow/wide dimensions considered by the management of the businesses listed in Table 6-1 in thinking about their strategic direction.

Developing a strategic direction is not merely a work exercise. The strategic direction serves as a directional beacon to nonmarketing as well as marketing personnel, shedding light on the breadth of activities they will undertake over a three- to five-year period. It also

Table 6-1. Dimensions of a business.

| COMPANY | STRATEGIC DIRECTION | |
	NARROW	WIDE
Gerber Products	Baby foods manufacturer	Child care business
J. P. Stevens	Textile manufacturer	Total home environment business
Bekins Company	Mover of household products	Relocation business

directs the range of products, services, and markets (objectives and strategies) you will explore.

Every organization, large or small, uses the strategic direction in planning for each division, department, and product line. In all cases, managers must ensure that the strategic direction is consistent with the highest-level corporate mission statement, appropriately modified.

Objectives and Goals

This section of the plan focuses on what should be accomplished over the planning period. Objectives are indicated in two forms. First, quantitative objectives are set for sales dollars and units, return on investment, profit, share of market, and similar measurements, usually mandated by the organization. The second set of objectives, the non-quantitative ones, cover:

- Upgrading dealer or distributor groups
- Expanding into secondary areas of distribution, reaching beyond the immediate customer to other links in the distribution chain
- Strengthening a market position in a specific market segment
- Building specialty products to penetrate a new market or to retain a dominant position in an existing market
- Improving market intelligence systems
- Focusing training actions within the organization or within customer organizations

- Launching new products or repositioning old ones
- Upgrading customer or technical services
- Improving the management of product, price, promotion, and distribution to optimize performance

These objectives demonstrate an interaction among business activities that drive the actions of both marketing and nonmarketing managers. The Mitsubishi case cited earlier in this chapter demonstrates the interaction of many of the above categories as the company sought to define and penetrate an unserved market niche for large-screen TVs.

Growth Strategies

Strategies are actions to achieve objectives. For each of the objectives stated in the Objectives and Goals section, it is appropriate to develop from three to five strategies.

Strategies include internal and external actions. *Internal* actions include marketing, manufacturing, research and development, distribution, pricing new and existing products, as well as packaging, customer services, sales activities, market research, and even organizational changes. *External* actions derive from the possibilities of joint ventures, new distribution networks, emerging market segments, licensing, exporting, and diversification.

The Procter & Gamble/Wal-Mart example in this chapter illustrates the application of some of these strategies.

Business Portfolio Plan

Based on the three previous sections of the Strategic Marketing Plan, a portfolio of products and markets will emerge. Generally, the wider the strategic direction, the broader the range of products and markets; conversely, the narrower the strategic direction, the more limited the assortment of products and markets. Figure 6-2 provides a convenient matrix to list (1) existing products in existing markets, (2) existing products in new markets, (3) new products in existing markets, and (4) new products in new markets. Each quadrant of the portfolio matrix should be filled in with a list of products, services, and markets. The matrix serves as a convenient organizer for viewing the scope of existing and new products and markets. After examining the portfolio, it is often necessary to revise portions of the preceding sections of the plan. For example, to conform to the number of new products shown and the types of markets identified, you may need to

Figure 6-2. Product/market portfolio matrix.

	Existing Products	New Products
Existing Markets	Market Penetration	Product Development
New Markets	Market Development	Diversification

fine-tune your objectives and indicate how the revised objectives will be achieved by indicating corresponding actions in the strategy section.

While Motorola had an existing line of electronic products to put into the appropriate section of the portfolio, its MicroTac cellular phone and the wristwatch pager fell into the new product segment. Similarly, Mitsubishi had its 35-inch TVs as existing products during its opening launch into the large-screen segment; but additional product development into 60-inch and 120-inch TVs expanded its portfolio into the other sections of the matrix.

This section of the chapter has reviewed the long-term portion of the Strategic Marketing Plan. For nonmarketing managers the lesson should be clear: all activities within a market-driven organization must be interrelated if competitive advantage is to be achieved. No longer can the polarizing effects of finance against marketing or distribution against sales exist. Collaboration through teamwork is the essential ingredient for success in developing and following the Strategic Marketing Plan.

As we have seen, planning is the mental process that is used to analyze environmental, industry, competitor, and customer factors. From that thought process a manager develops a strategic direction and identifies long- and short-term objectives consisting of quantitative and nonquantitative outcomes. The manager also formulates strategies related to internal and external actions and designs a business portfolio consisting of existing and new products and markets.

CHAPTER 7

Developing a Tactical Marketing Plan

In this chapter we discuss the second part of the Strategic Marketing Plan, the short-term tactical marketing plan.

First, let's review the grand design of the Strategic Marketing Plan. Because of the difficulty of making accurate long-term (three- to five-year) projections, the *strategic* portion of the Strategic Marketing Plan, discussed in Chapter 6, is more general than the short-term (one-year) *tactical* marketing plan. The strategic focus is used for establishing organizational, market, product, human resources, and financial objectives as well as determining strategies, which may take considerable time to execute.

Focusing on a business unit's or a product line's strategic direction orients the manager in terms of economic conditions, shifts in market patterns, trends in customer buying behavior, and alignment of competitors' positions. It also helps to forecast sales trends of various products, anticipate new product lines, and present broad objectives and strategies.

During the strategic planning period, a manager has a chance to make strategy decisions that will impact a company's prospects for growth. More precisely, the strategic part of the plan establishes priorities, while the tactical part implements them. If, for example, a company wishes to develop a new product, it must plan how to market it several years in advance so that funds and facilities can be provided. If the decision is made in enough time, the budget, personnel, and other departments of the company can provide for the extra money, people, and other resources in their annual plans.

AT&T Data Systems Group, a division of AT&T, illustrates these principles.

CASE EXAMPLE

AT&T Data Systems Group, as part of its long-term strategic objectives, planned to establish joint ventures with computer hardware and software companies that could supply networking systems and expertise that was lacking from its parent, AT&T.

Intense competition forced the group's managers to learn quickly that thinking they could depend solely on the corporate AT&T name to land a customer created a false sense of security, particularly in regard to their giant competitors, such as IBM and Digital Equipment. Managers worked with field salespeople to identify market niches that represented long-term growth. They focused on customer problems and planned differentiated product offerings, whether generated internally or through the joint ventures.

They also selected for joint venture only those companies that had specific networking skills focused on those market segments and target customers identified in the long-term plan. Thus, implementing the strategies required customizing solutions to customers' problems, regardless of whose equipment or software was used.

The effectiveness of the strategy is measured by the performance. The AT&T group landed computer orders from American Airlines, Firestone Tire & Rubber, Pizza Hut, Chrysler Financial, and United Parcel Service. The AT&T Data Systems' managers learned that establishing meaningful corporate partnerships and offering individualized solutions to customer problems as formulas for their success requires strategic vision, strategic thinking—and strategic marketing planning.

What information goes into the strategic part of the Strategic Marketing Plan? The following is a summary of possible objectives and strategies based on the situation we have described:[1]

1. Establish joint ventures with hardware and software companies that have systems capabilities and networking expertise that

---

1. These statements are not the actual plans of AT&T but are interpretations based on their situation.

AT&T lacks. These alliances should provide rapid, customized solutions to customers' problems.

2. Focus on target markets where AT&T's networking skills can succeed. Avoid a direct confrontation with larger competitors by seeking market niches that afford a competitive advantage.

3. Encourage an entrepreneurial spirit throughout the group. Within corporate guidelines, cut free from the bureaucratic culture; stimulate the flow of innovative ideas from all managerial levels and the field salesforce; encourage a competitive attitude, a creative capability, and a desire to win. Use whatever approach works, intensifying the internal communications network, honoring achievers individually, or offering financial incentives.

4. Where new hardware and software systems from the joint ventures create differentiation, rapidly and vigorously promote the competitive advantage.

5. Shape strategies and tactics at the deepest levels of the organization, involving those close to the field and to the customer. The strategies and tactics help to develop innovative dealer relationships, permit pricing flexibility, and identify value-added services that salespeople can use to close deals.

6. Exploit opportunities by educating and motivating marketing and nonmarketing employees to implement strategies and tactics day in and day out.

Tactical plans, on the other hand, incorporate considerably more detail. As operational plans, they serve to achieve objectives within a concentrated period of time. Thus, they link the strategic and tactical parts of the plan into a single planning entity.

The tactical marketing plan section of the Strategic Marketing Plan is longer and more detailed than the section containing long-range plans. It spells out budget allocations, priorities, target objectives, tactics, and dates for completion. These items are organized by function and the person responsible for each action or activity. The tactical marketing plan emphasizes specific products as well as production, promotion, and sales objectives.

In many cases, the tactical marketing plan is accompanied by a contingency plan to be used in the event a strategy or tactic has to be altered in midstream. The short-term plan thus represents the practical implementation of the company's, division's, or product line's long-range plan.

Using the AT&T Data Systems Group tactical actions as our focus, we now present a tactical marketing plan. Observe how these actions complement the strategic part of the plan.

1. Educate nonmarketing personnel to the concepts, skills, and vocabulary of competitive marketing strategy through a series of intensive quarterly training sessions.
Intent: Prepare managers to sustain the competitive intensity and to adopt a customer-driven orientation.

2. Establish, within the first quarter, three multifunctional teams of middle managers and teach them how to develop strategy plans and manage opportunities within targeted niches. Authorize them to seek alliances with companies that can provide expertise and networking systems to create competitive advantage.
Intent: Obtain middle managers' buy-in so they can take responsibility for implementing their own functional plans and thereby encourage harmonious relationships with other operational units.

3. By the second quarter, refine the group's planning system linking the longer-term strategic vision at the senior management level with the lowest echelons for implementation.
Intent: Use a common planning system to communicate strategy, unify the group, and initiate strategic thinking among all levels of managers.

4. Begin monthly meetings to orient senior managers to the need to instill market-driven, customer-driven attitudes throughout their respective units.
Intent: Create definable, repeatable processes so that managers at all levels can understand markets, select opportunities, articulate customer requirements, and identify solutions.

COMPONENTS OF THE TACTICAL MARKETING PLAN

Using the AT&T example to illustrate both the strategic and tactical portions of the plan, we now detail the content of the tactical marketing plan. Figure 7-1 highlights the lower row of boxes representing the tactical marketing plan, which consists of situation analysis, marketing opportunities, objectives, strategies, and financial controls.

Figure 7-1. Strategic marketing plan.

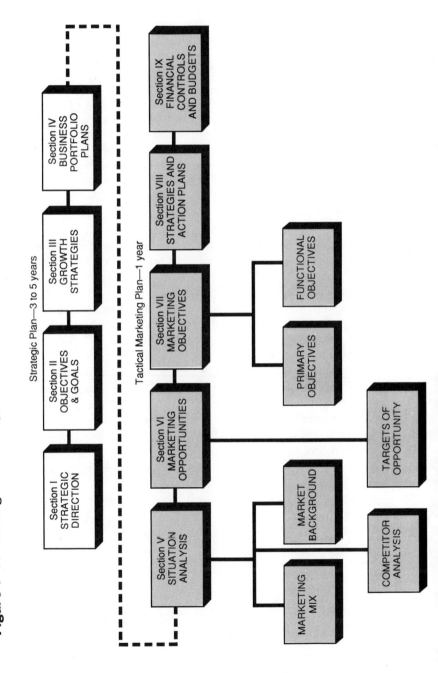

Situation Analysis

Situation analysis consists of three parts: marketing mix, competitive situation, and market background. While there is a good deal of drudgery connected with gathering these data, they are essential to provide quality input in the sections that follow.

Marketing Mix. In this part, you describe in factual terms where your company, business unit, or product line stands in relation to the marketing mix (product, price, promotion, and distribution). Data on various functions are compiled for at least three years to provide a historical perspective. These functions include sales history, market position (usually expressed by share-of-market figures), and indicators of where the product is in its life cycle (introduction, growth, maturity, or decline).

Competitive Situation. The next part profiles the competition according to overall strengths and weaknesses related to organizational structure, management competence, and financial resources. You may also make comparisons by product quality and performance, packaging uniqueness, service capability, pricing strategies, promotion resources, salesforce effectiveness, and distribution coverage. (See Chapter 3 on market intelligence for additional factors connected with competitive analysis.)

Market Background. The final part of the situation analysis focuses on the behavioral aspects of customers and prospects in a changing and competitive environment. This information is important, for it serves as a foundation on which to develop the opportunities, objectives, and strategies that follow. It also highlights any gaps in your knowledge of your markets and suggests what market intelligence is needed to make effective decisions.

Included in this part is information about your customers at various stages of the distribution chain. For example, if you sell through intermediaries, such as distributors or dealers, those intermediaries are profiled according to sales performance, territorial coverage, and growth performance. You also need to profile *their* customers' product usage and buying behavior to obtain greater insight about those final users.

Getting closer to the end-use customer is as relevant to the business-to-business producer as it is to the consumer packaged goods company, even if only a component of a final product is supplied. Thus, to the extent possible, examine your *customers' behavior* to stay close to changing market needs—and ahead of your competitors.

The more information you have about customers, the better. For example, you should record frequency and magnitude of products used, consumption by geographic region of the products used, and customer characteristics (demographics, buying motivation at various decision-making levels, attitudes toward your company, and level of awareness of your company's products).

Marketing Opportunities

As you study the facts presented in the situation analysis and examine your strengths and weaknesses, you will discover opportunities in various aspects of the marketing operation. In this section of the marketing plan, you have the luxury of brainstorming and considering fresh options. It may be useful to convene a planning group and consider all possibilities that can expand your coverage of existing markets and lay the groundwork for entering new markets. In this section you should also prioritize your opportunities and develop them into objectives to be presented in the next section of the plan.

Targets of Opportunity. The presentation of opportunities can be broken down as follows:

1. *Present markets.* Consider the opportunities for expanding present markets through:

- Cultivating new users
- Displacing competition from key accounts or market niches
- Increasing product usage among customers
- Redefining market segments and reformatting the product to meet new customer requirements
- Repositioning the product to give it a fresh appeal, through either enhancements or add-on services

2. *Customers.* Determine the best opportunities for:

- Improving or expanding channels of distribution
- Providing pricing deals

- Focusing product promotions to target those customers or geographical areas that will yield the greatest return
- Enhancing customer services

3. *Growth markets.* Identify markets that contain growth potential. These markets may be those that are emerging and have potential as consumers of an existing or modified product, those neglected by competitors, or those poorly served in the past. Examine market segments by industry, customer size, geographic location, or product application.

4. *Product and service development.* Single out the immediate and long-term opportunities for product development and innovation in the following areas:

- Adding new products to the line
- Diversifying into new or related products or product lines
- Modifying or redesigning products
- Developing innovative packaging
- Introducing new customer or technical services

Marketing Objectives

Having reported relevant factual data in the situation analysis, interpreted their meaning, and converted them into opportunities, you should now select your objectives for the short term (usually defined as twelve months). The objectives, which should be both realistic and attainable, should be divided into three parts: primary, functional, and nonproduct.

Primary Objectives. These objectives relate to product-line sales, measured in dollars, units/customers, market share, profit margins, return on investment, or any other quantitative measurements required by the organization.

Functional Objectives. In this section you make specific statements about *what* is going to happen over a twelve-month period, based on the previous sections of the plan.

You should clearly state objectives for products, services, and markets, using all or some of the categories listed in this section. The categories suggest a comprehensive range of possibilities; you should review them all but select those that you can realistically deal with during the time period covered in the plan. Notice how the categories parallel those addressed in the sections dealing with long-term objectives, growth strategies, and the business portfolio.

Suggested categories for functional objectives are:

- Quality
- Development
- Modification
- Differentiation
- Deletion
- Segmentation
- Pricing
- Promotion (sales, sales promotion, advertising, publicity)
- Distribution channels
- Logistics (warehousing and physical distribution)
- Packaging
- Service
- Other

Nonproduct Objectives. These objectives support the functional objectives and are also reviewed for selecting objectives. Observe, in particular, how many nonmarketing activities are involved:

- Target accounts (by segment, product application, or for strategic importance within an industry)
- Manufacturing (quality, flexibility, performance, or product enhancements)
- Credit
- Technical sales activities
- Research and development
- Training
- Human resources development
- Other

Strategies and Action Plans (Tactics)

After selecting your marketing objectives, you should restate the product and nonproduct objectives indicated in the previous sections. Then describe the course of action planned to achieve each objective, along with target dates and individual(s) assigned to the task.

Financial Controls

Having completed the design phase of the plan, determine how to monitor its execution. Establish procedures for both control (comparing actual and planned figures) and review (deciding whether planned figures should be adjusted or other corrective measures taken). (Details of financial controls, such as budgeting, are given in a later section of this chapter.)

The overall procedure is as follows:

1. *Establish Controls.* This function requires setting up feedback mechanisms relating to timing, responsibility, content, and method of presentation. Controls exist in most organizations, typically in the form of budgets and other periodic reports; if this applies to your organization, use or modify what exists. You should also process comparative data related to objectives; they can provide warning signals by highlighting variances of planned versus actual figures.

2. *Review Procedures.* Establish time schedules and determine the levels of management that should participate in the review procedures. Then determine which policies or objectives should be reviewed for possible revision in light of long- and short-term market conditions and competitive actions.

We have now completed our overview of the tactical marketing plan. It combines with the strategic plan to form a complete Strategic Marketing Plan. The total plan is designed to be an operational, hands-on blueprint to guide activities. However, good judgment should prevail. The plan should be flexible enough to adapt to market conditions; market conditions cannot adapt to the plan.

The intent of this planning review is to demonstrate the need, indeed the necessity, for nonmarketing managers to participate and actively contribute to developing the Strategic Marketing Plan.

The framework of a marketing plan must be firmly based on reality, and marketing objectives must be reasonable and achievable. The major aid to setting realistic objectives is demand analysis, which predicts both the potential demand for a product and the company's potential share of market.

DEMAND ANALYSIS

The purpose of a demand analysis is to determine which products the company can sell and at what price. First, sales of the product are forecast; then the probable reactions of competitors are predicted. These steps are important, especially to smaller companies that could be wiped out if their estimates of demand and competitive activity are not accurate.

Demand analysis can be used with totally new products, with newly refined products, with old products in new packages, or with value-added products containing new features. In each case, the purpose of the analysis is to anticipate the share of the particular market the product can expect to receive.

Estimating Demand

Most products are similar in some ways to existing products made by other companies. Product categories can assist managers in determining how many products of which type can be sold in the market by their company. Changes in demand for most products are related to shifts in income at the consumer level, to changes of prices of related products, or to changes in consumer attitudes. To a large degree, each of these factors is measurable.

Generally, products are said to be either relatively *elastic* or relatively *inelastic*. The more stable a product's sales, the more it is said to be inelastic. In other words, the more consistently customers purchase a product irrespective of its price, the more the marketer can predict its future demand. Staple items, emergency items, and certain prestige items fall into this category. At the opposite end of the scale are products whose sales vary greatly with shifts in price (elastic demand). Such items are substantially dependent on changing economic conditions as predictors of sales.

For most products, the probable quantity that can be sold is relatively predictable over time, as is the probable impact of any change in economic conditions on the items' sales. It is important to analyze the relationship of one product to other products as an aid to predicting the elasticity of its sales. For example, sales of large cars are affected by the price of gasoline, the general economic situation, and the indebtedness of the buying public. Furthermore, it is generally recognized that if steel (or plastic) prices rise substantially, forcing auto costs up, certain car models will be priced out of the range of many former customers.

A demand analysis indicates only possibilities, not the final solution. It might, for example, show that several products have equal chances of success. It is at this point that the manager must make a decision. Resources are always limited, and managers cannot pursue every possible source of action. They must decide among alternatives.

TECHNIQUES OF DECISION MAKING

Some managers believe that marketers feed information into computers and then, solely on the basis of mathematical computations, make decisions of whether and how to market a product. Mathematical computations do aid in making decisions, but the decision-making process requires more. It is a skill that involves determining alternatives, comparing their probable outcomes, and deciding on one path. Factual data, experience, and intuition all play a part in the process.

The best way to make a decision is to define the problem, determine its underlying causes, develop alternative modes of action, and select the best alternative. The better the issue is defined, the stronger the possibility of making the correct decision.

In considering which of two alternatives to choose, a company should look not only at the potential profit involved but also at the potential indirect effects of the decision for the company. Can a product, for instance, help a company enter a new market later on? Does it give the company prestige, which is valuable in other ways? Would the product's cancellation or the reduction of its production have adverse effects on other segments of the company's position, perhaps, for example, leaving production capability unused? These are only a few of the questions that must be asked while making a decision.

Types of Decisions

There are two basic types of decisions: repetitive and one-time. Repetitive decisions recur on a relatively frequent basis. They can be handled routinely once a decision process has been established; because the alternatives are static for a time, the decision need not be rethought but becomes a procedure to be used until the alternatives, the company environment, the nature of the marketplace, or other factors change.

The ordering of office supplies is a simple example of a routine decision. If a company has found that it uses four packages of computer paper a day and that it takes three weeks to receive a new order of the paper, it can simply reorder when the supply on hand is down to sixty packages (three weeks, or fifteen business days, times four).

Managers need not rethink this decision every time the company runs out of paper.

Complex situations can be readily solved once they have been carefully studied. If a company has enjoyed a 20 percent share of a staple-product market over a period of years and competitors are not introducing innovations, it is safe to predict market potential for the product for the next year or two. If conditions were to change—for example, if a an old competitor, with an infusion of cash resulting from a merger, were to take over a larger share of the market—then the decision would no longer be a repetitive one, and it would then become necessary to establish a whole new decision-making process.

One-time, or nonrecurring, decisions are a different matter. They involve problems that have not come up before, at least not in exactly the same context. Therefore, the company must go through the decision-making process, which can involve data gathering, risk estimates, gain or loss projections, and review of the fit between alternatives and planning objectives.

Many approaches to decision making have been developed; we shall consider the methods commonly used by managers. Many of these techniques were devised for large companies, but small companies can often use them in modified form. In any case, awareness of alternative approaches should prove helpful to companies of any size.

Models

A model is a miniature or replica of an issue under study. Architects construct small-scale models of proposed buildings; TV weather reporters use models in the form of charts of the weather pattern. Business managers use models to help in their planning. A model of the economy for the past year can be shown on charts and graphs; a model of the growth of sales of a product over the past five or ten years can be shown on a single chart. The intent in each case is to present a condition in perspective so the viewer can gain insight into the total situation.

Managers use models to study all the possible alternatives before arriving at a decision. Models are safeguards; they help ensure that no alternative is overlooked. Model building may be considered a prerequisite to decision making.

In the following discussion, we consider several of the most common models for business planning: role playing, computerized simulation, and game theory. All these models are simulations. Simulations artificially duplicate the reactions of competitors and the marketplace in general to a given product and its marketing approach. They attempt to recreate situations and the interplay among the people involved in them.

Role Playing. Team members can participate in decision making by acting out roles representing the company's rivals. They are given as much data as possible about their company role, including information about the competitor's resources and personnel. They do not have to react in any set way to an event; for example, if the aim of the simulation is to determine how competitors might react to a strong promotional effort, participants decide on a course of action based on their personal opinion of the best way to solve the problem.

Although at first glance role playing might seem too simplistic to be useful, it enables the company to evaluate a plan from all angles and alternatives. At the same time, staff members gain valuable experience in making decisions, even if in theoretical situations. Role playing is also useful in personnel training situations. Case studies show that once people begin to respond emotionally to a hypothetical situation, they carry out the role they are playing as though the circumstances were real.

Computerized Simulation. Computerized simulation is a more sophisticated form of role playing in which the computer plays all the roles. Pertinent data are fed into the computer, which is then programmed to compute certain business actions under a number of variables—changing business conditions, company pricing changes, or new product introductions, for example. The data may be complex, but the computer can project the reactions of competition and the marketplace for the many courses of action the company is considering.

The advantage of using the computer for this task is its unique ability to handle such complex instructions quickly—and to observe the results of decisions, permitting a more detailed set of planning variables to be included in the experiment. The success or failure of such simulations depends upon the accuracy and completeness of the data fed into the computer.

Small companies can rarely afford the expense of preparing a specific computerized simulation. However, generic programs of other firms are available for individual or group use. Members of some trade associations can make use of industry models, which provide more detail concerning the probable situation within the industry in general. Companies can use this information to project their own alternatives, helping to study the probable impact of other companies' decisions on their own actions.

Game Theory. Game theory is another model for predicting how competitors will react to a company's marketing plan. Unlike role playing, however, it is based solely on historical data; the participants in the game are not allowed free rein in their reactions.

Game theory argues that the history of how competitors have reacted to similar situations in the past is a good indication of how they will react to future conditions. If past data show that every time a company has placed a full-page advertisement in the local newspaper, a competitor has placed a similar ad, chances are that the competitor will repeat this reaction if the first company places another ad. This type of information is useful not only to these two companies but to the entire industry. The confrontation forces a chain reaction. Small firms can begin to predict within what price ranges they can act with relatively little risk and at what point larger firms will feel pressed and respond.

Like role playing, game theory simulation can be computerized. A vast amount of historical data is fed into a computer, which is programmed to predict reaction to alternative plans according to historical precedent. The following axioms of strategy have grown out of game theory:

- The more aggressive your marketing practices when entering a market, the more you risk having competitors harden their resistance and turn against you. Even if you succeed in winning the market, you will profit less from your efforts.
- If you and a competitor are evenly matched in resources but your rival holds a strong market position too costly to dislodge, even with a major marketing effort, you should develop attractive alternatives as the quickest way of loosening its hold. You thereby provide the competitor an easy way out of the market should it wish to shift resources to a less combative environment.
- The more intent you are in securing a market position entirely on your own terms, the stiffer the obstacles in your path and the more likely competitors will try to reverse what you have achieved.

- While the tools of marketing—promotion, field selling, distribution, product development—are physical acts, their direction is a mental process. The better your strategy, the easier you will gain the upper hand and the less it will cost you.

These and other considerations can be reduced to formulas that test the probability of actions based on prestated conditions. Small firms can make use of these principles and can also keep track of competitors' reactions under various economic and competitive circumstances, enabling them to predict their competitors' future actions with a fair degree of accuracy.

DECISION THEORY

We have analyzed the demand for the product and have discovered an approach to reducing complex problems methodically so they can be studied for decision making. Decision theory is not a theory in the strictest sense but is a method of reaching decisions. One particularly useful method for decision making is probability theory.

Probability Theory

After managers have developed models of what their competition is likely to do, they are ready to weigh the probable outcomes of their decisions. To do so, they often use an approach known as *probability theory*.

The general principle of probability theory requires that each probability be assigned a specific value. Perhaps a company is wondering whether a competitor will introduce a product to the market during the next year. After looking at the available data, planners may assign a probability of 60 percent to that occurrence. If the event does happen, a probability might be placed on the loss of sales likely to be suffered by the planner's product. It might be determined that, based on what occurred the last time the competitor introduced a new product, there is an 80 percent chance that sales will be cut by 10 percent but a probability of only 20 percent that they will be cut as much as 25 percent. These probabilities, along with other variables, serve as a useful guide to evaluating risks and alternatives.

Decision Criteria

To a large extent, decision making depends on the manager's own attitudes. No matter how carefully a company has studied the problem, competitors' actions and the precise nature of the economy remain uncertain to some extent. The manager may therefore either take an optimistic or a pessimistic view of how things will go. In operations research, the terms for these alternative views are *maximax* or *maximin*. A third variation is called *minimax*.

Place yourself in the position of a manager who knows that, as a result of production decisions already made, the supply of product is about to arrive for distribution. Let's also assume that the manager simply does not know which pricing approaches will work best. What is known is that each criterion will result in a predictable profit or loss. That is, if the price is based on the criterion of optimism and conditions prove to be favorable, the company will make $80,000; if the situation is mildly favorable, the profit will be $20,000. If the estimate of the situation is incorrect and the results are unfavorable, the company will lose $30,000. On the other hand, if the pricing decision is based on a pessimistic estimate, the outcomes will be $20,000, $15,000, and $12,000, respectively.

Under the criterion of optimism, or maximax, the decision maker looks at the bright side of events, making the assumption that rivals will be unsuccessful in their competition and that the economy will hold firm. Therefore, the manager decides to place a high sales price on the products. If the decision is correct, profits will be maximized ($80,000). On the other hand, if the company's position or the economy has been misjudged, the company will suffer the greatest possible loss (−$30,000). Not only will the company have overproduced the merchandise but, because of the high prices placed on its products, competitors' products will appear more attractive to the cost-conscious customers of a depressed market. The criterion of optimism leads to the most extreme position for the decision maker. Chances of potential profits and potential risks are maximized. The company will either be very well off or bankrupt. This, then, is the nature of aggressive, optimistic planning, or maximax.

Under the criterion of pessimism, or maximin, the assumption is that all decisions will go against the company. Even if indications are that the competition will not introduce a new product and that economic conditions will remain strong during the planning period, caution is the watchword. Here, the decision maker permits the goods to be sold at low prices, the goal being a minimal profit but a reduced risk of not moving the merchandise because of high prices. Further, according to this line of reasoning, customers might be attracted from competitors by the low price.

Under this pessimistic, or maximin, approach, the company will earn a moderate profit ($20,000) if conditions are good—but it will have lost the chance to make large profits; a company operating under the maximax approach will have preempted them. However, under adverse circumstances such as a recession or unexpected competition, the company will still receive a modest profit, and it will be far better off than it would have been had it attempted to operate under conditions of optimism which, in fact, did not develop.

Some managers, unable to choose between maximax and maximin approaches, employ the criterion of regret, or minimax. This is not another approach to decision making; it is a result of fear of choosing either pole of approach. The manager decides on compromise, in our illustration a moderate price, which will most likely cause the manager a minimum of regret. That is, the company will neither lose heavily nor, of course, make much money even under the best of circumstances. In planning, compromise is important; however, companies that wish to grow and maintain a strong competitive position must take some bold action. If management is afraid to make effective risk-taking decisions, it jeopardizes the company's growth potential. A look at Table 7-1 presents the criteria with projected outcomes for the illustration we have given.

One other probability-based approach to decision making should be noted: the La Place criterion, or criterion of rationality, is based on estimates of probability of events. This criterion is very useful if the

Table 7-1. Decision Criteria: Product Gain or Loss Over Time Period

ECONOMIC CONDITIONS	OPTIMISM (MAXIMAX) $	PESSIMISM (MAXIMIN) $	MINIMUM REGRET (MINIMAX) $
Favorable	80,000	20,000	30,000
Mild	20,000	15,000	16,000
Unfavorable	(30,000)	12,000	5,000

appropriate information is available but is restricted to large firms because of its complexity.

RESOURCE ALLOCATION

Once you establish objectives and specific product plans, you must determine and assess the types of company resources needed to implement a specific strategy. Money, personnel, and production resources must all be considered. Overcommitment of resources remains a major danger, leaving no room for later adjustments and contingencies in the plan.

Planning cannot take place without some consideration of resource allocation. Allocation models can help the manager in this task.

Allocation Models

Allocation models are intended to help the manager determine how to use limited resources for the business's maximum benefit. The models plot the allocation of funds or other resources in various ways and show the probable results of various possible allocations.

Allocation models serve two purposes. First, they indicate how resources should be channeled to effect specific marketing plans. Second, they clarify the financial soundness of each allocation, enabling the manager to see how to allocate resources to eliminate as many risks of financial failure as possible and to gain the greatest return on investment. Allocation models are most helpful in budget planning.

BUDGETS

Planning requires facts, which are typically presented in unit, dollar, return on investment, share of market, and a variety of other quantitative measurements. This information is usually provided in budgetary form. Marketing, as only one function of a business, must be assessed in relation to allocation needs of other departments. The budgeting system operates at two distinct yet complementary levels: at the company level and the operating unit level.

The companywide budget estimates resources and projects needs for the total company. Operating unit budgets, which are prepared by each unit, are part of the financial controls section of the strategic marketing plan and present a total picture for each unit's operations to senior management. If the total company budget does not support the unit budget, the unit must adjust its figures. As with other departments, marketing must base its programs on overall corporate plans and limit itself to the resources available during the planning period.

Types of Budgets

Budgets assist not only in planning but also in implementation, scheduling, and control. Our concern here is with budgets only as part of the planning sequence. Corporate planning budgets usually begin with statements of (1) projected income and expenses, (2) projected financial condition, (3) projected cash flow, and (4) projected capital expenditures.

Statement of Projected Income and Expenses. An analysis and statement of income from sales is basic to the planning process. Forecasts of sales, based on the economy and competitors' actions, come early in the planning process. In the budget, sales figures are organized by product and territory and provide a foundation for estimating income for the planning period. This income figure is then balanced with detailed expense figures showing cost of goods sold, expense of operations, and other appropriate expense categories. The statement must be clear enough to enable planners to see the relationship of sales to expense items.

Statement of Projected Financial Condition. The primary function of this budget statement is to indicate where the tightest financial resource problems will be. Projected monthly or quarterly balance sheets can serve this purpose. Knowing where the crunch will come permits special attention to the crucial periods of the planning period.

Statement of Projected Cash Flow. Cash flow statements are estimates of cash use requirements over the planning period. They take data from the other budgets and place them in a format that permits management to observe the company's current position.

Before any revenue is received from a particular product, raw and processed materials for the product's manufacture must be purchased, advertising paid for, and sales calls made. During this period the company must have enough money on hand to proceed with the next stage. The cash flow statement tells the company how much money it has on hand by projecting expenses and receipts during each month. It allows management to see how much money is needed for how long to keep the company from running into trouble. It also permits management to note if projections are not being fulfilled, requiring quick action from management to adjust the plan and strategy.

The cash flow statement is perhaps the most vital of the budgets. It focuses on what top management and marketing management need to know. It also represents one of the easiest ways for management to determine which projects it is practical to propose for the planning period and which should be dropped to fulfill the company's financial goals.

Statement of Projected Capital Expenditures. A company may decide to invest money in capital expenditures such as building improvement, new equipment, and other one-time improvement costs. The capital expenditure statement presents the costs and anticipated returns of such proposed expenses in dollar amounts.

Budgets and Strategic Marketing Planning

In preparing departmental budgets, the planning team must estimate sales and indicate profit probability. Members of the company review these estimates, developing a total picture for the company. Then the marketing department is given expenditure estimates for the planning period. At this point the team must adjust budgets to match the amount provided in the master budget. Of course, it may discuss problems with top management and make some adjustments in the amount allocated for marketing. But the marketing budget is determined by the total company picture; strategic marketing planning must be adjusted to fit into the total picture. The typical marketing budget includes the following specific items and subbudgets:

1. *Sales budget.* The sales budget lists sales by products, prices, territory, and estimated returns.

2. *Inventory and materials budget.* This budget states the inventory necessary to achieve the anticipated sales levels for the planning period. It includes estimates of materials and supplies necessary to fill orders promptly.

3. *Cost of goods sold estimate.* This statement includes material

costs, labor costs, and manufacturing expenses. The costs of goods sold, probably the most used estimator, is usually calculated before the rest of the budget.

4. *Sales and administrative expense estimates.* This category may be broken down into two separate budgets, for it covers independent categories: sales and sales support expenses, such as wages and promotional support expenditures, and administrative costs of marketing. These costs tend to be high and should be monitored closely on the basis of sales results. Many companies find that they have allocated insufficient funds for effective promotion and consequently are in the unfortunate position of having made a substantial commitment in support of a product without receiving the anticipated benefits of sales. Perhaps worse, they have lost the chance to spend the money on other profit-producing alternatives.

5. *Research and product development budget.* Research is one of the keys to future growth. Budgets should be large enough to supply a continuous flow of product if marketing is to function in identifying and fulfilling market needs. However, judgment must prevail in developing research budgets. For example, is the research basic, with marketable products available many years into the future, or is it applied research, with the expectation of new or modified products rolling out in the foreseeable future and with great frequency? Is there enough existing technology and expertise within the organization to conduct adequate research in keeping with industry standards? Or should the research budget be modest, with funds applied instead to beefing up marketing budgets? Can new products be acquired through licensing, joint ventures, or other forms of alliances?

In summary, planning each type of budget requires considerable effort, but it is necessary if they are to provide the data to allow appropriate use of resources. However, no matter how good a budget is, it cannot foresee every contingency. Therefore, all budgets should allow for funds for emergency use. Such funds not only provide insurance against sudden reverses but permit the flexibility necessary to take advantage of unexpected opportunities. The precise level of leeway in a budget depends on the industry and corporate situation.

THE PLANNING AUDIT

An audit typically reviews the company's accounting to determine whether the firm has complied with tax law. It should provide assurance that funds have been expended honestly and appropriately.

A company may also decide to conduct an audit to determine whether expenditures achieve anticipated goals and objectives. This sort of review is known as a planning audit. As with the other types of audits, it is a check—this time, a check on the plan's performance.

Establishing a Planning Audit

A planning audit uses predetermined benchmarks to gauge performance at various checkpoints; it compares planned objectives against actual objectives for a given period. If, for example, projections led managers to expect a product line to sell at the rate of 100,000 units in the first three months, while the audit shows that actual sales amounted to only 60,000 units, there is cause for concern. The audit has served its purpose; now management can adapt its plans to fit the altered situation. If the planned and the actual figures come close to agreement, the plan is reinforced, and management may turn its attention to other problems.

Planning audits, particularly those that deal with marketing areas, are not perfect, but they are helpful in determining the present state of the marketing plan. Some of the checkpoints at which you want the planning audit to measure performance include the following:

1. *The Strategic Marketing Plan—strategic section*. Assess if the company or the operating unit is holding to its strategic direction. Evaluate progress toward reaching long-term objectives and strategies. Examine if external conditions are fully surveyed by considering such factors as the environment, industry, customers, and competitors; determine if internal factors relating to organizational efficiency, financial strength, distribution, service, product development, and sales and promotional efforts are objectively reviewed.

2. *The Strategic Marketing Plan—tactical section*. Examine progress toward exploiting opportunities related to markets and products. Determine if any competitive actions, either aggressive or passive, are creating problems or opportunities. Measure to see if the short-term objectives are being achieved. Review to see if existing tactics continue to be appropriate for reaching all objectives or if any need modification. Conduct the audit by measuring sales, market share, sales-to-expense ratios, financial objectives, and customer attitudes.

3. *Profitability control*. Compare actual results with planned finan-

cial objectives and with general corporate guidelines. Specifically, go beyond the overall numbers and measure profitability by product, market segment, customer purchase patterns, territory, and distribution channel.

4. *Efficiency control.* Using the customer-oriented marketing concept as an organizational priority, evaluate efficiency of efforts toward achieving customer satisfaction by surveying product quality, customer service, salesforce productivity, advertising and sales promotion effectiveness, and logistical efficiency (physical handling of product or service, order processing, warehousing).

PREPARING THE SCHEDULES

A plan should be broken down into schedules, and the timing of each element should be spelled out. Every expenditure must be calculated. Once the Strategic Marketing Plan has been structured in this way, it can serve as a guide for the planning period as well as for control.

Companies utilize many type of schedules. Timetables, cash flow statements, graphs, and charts are all important schedules, and there are sophisticated computerized techniques which provide even more detailed information. The following discussion deals with the more common approaches to scheduling.

Timetable of Deadlines

Scheduling thrives on deadlines. These deadlines are predetermined points by which certain goals must be reached, or at least certain actions taken. Let us consider briefly two types of deadlines.

Data Deadlines. Data deadlines are used for audit, adjustment, and control of the plan, setting specified times for collecting data. Many types of data may be collected on a deadline basis, including monthly sales records, quarterly income and expense statements, inventory statements, sales expense statements, quarterly balance sheets, and economic, competitive, and industry data.

The purpose of the deadline is to provide a continuing flow of on-time, pertinent information to avoid crises, correct problems, or pursue opportunities. This, in turn, should result in keeping senior management informed and should provide an ongoing opportunity to restudy the plan if it is shown to be faulty. Deadlines tend to make the management team strive to achieve its projected objectives prior to the due date.

Action Deadlines. Action deadlines define the dates by which specific actions should take place. They represent dates for some important move planned in advance by management. Here are some of the typical action deadlines for marketing managers:

1. *Physical events*
Shipping dates: Merchandise must be shipped by a certain date to be on the shelves in time for a holiday shopping event or, in some situations, to preempt a competitor's product entry.

Merchandise markdown dates: Perhaps management wants to take advantage of a special bargain day that ties into a national holiday; or perhaps it has determined that this is the best time to mark down merchandise to get the jump on competition or it needs to solve a cash flow problem.

Cancellation of production dates: Management has decided that if sales do not improve by this date, it will cancel production.

Warehouse clearance dates: Warehouse space might be needed for new merchandise by a specified date.

2. *Implementation events*
Advertising campaign dates: It has been determined that a particular period will be most effective for the campaign.

Extension or cancellation of production dates: If the product is doing better than expected, production will be increased; if worse, it will be canceled.

Dates to purchase under discount: This might be the best time to purchase needed equipment.

Alteration of plan implementation: Management has decided that this is the deadline for implementation of the original plan; if things aren't working out, alternative procedures must be adopted.

Each of these deadlines involves specific actions or decisions to be taken by the company; to bypass any one of them inadvertently would impose an unexpected hardship on the company. Deadline timetables are particularly useful for small companies. Indeed, they alone may provide sufficient control for management in monitoring its plan. For larger organizations, however, deadlines form only the first step in plan scheduling.

GUIDES TO EFFECTIVE PLANNING

The celebrated U.S. army general George S. Patton once stated, "One does not plan and then try to make circumstances fit the plans. One tries to make plans fit the circumstances." This wise advice applies to the sphere of global competitive marketing as well as to the military.

Making planning work, and specifically the type of planning discussed in this and the previous chapter, requires a market orientation. That means maintaining an outward view of circumstances relating the environment, industry, customers, and competitors and then adapting the plan to those circumstances. Managers can use the following guidelines to understand how strategic marketing planning works and how nonmarketing managers can contribute to its success:

1. *Make the plan fit market circumstances.* Keep an outward focus. That is what strategic direction, the first step of the Strategic Marketing Plan, intends to accomplish. But actual market conditions can blur the vision unless information—or more precisely, market intelligence—clarifies the circumstances. This topic is discussed in chapters 3 and 4.

2. *Develop top-down and bottom-up participation in planning by line and staff marketing and nonmarketing managers.* Employ the multifunctional team approach for each major product line or market segment. Such participation ensures a maximum input of strategic thinking by those individuals—particularly the line managers—who have to execute the plan. The multidirectional information flow has the additional benefit of permitting reliable communications to take place.

3. *Enlist the support of senior management.* At times senior management tends to create communications barriers with planning teams, either unintentionally because of external activities absorbing their attention or intentionally because of a hands-off management style. However, encouraging active support by senior management is required, since ultimately it is accountable for achieving overall corporate objectives. In line with obtaining support, it is appropriate to tailor the presentation of the plan to the characteristics of the key managers. The plan is a "product" to be sold to management for the

purpose of gaining support and obtaining funds; therefore, deal with the natural styles of managers. For example, if many statistics are required for credibility, provide them. If brief written summaries along with extensive verbal commentary work best, provide them. If graphic displays provide the visual impact that puts across the key ideas, present them.

4. *Keep planning uncomplicated.* Make the planning process simple. Avoid encumbering it with complex systems and exhaustive planning manuals that complicate the planning process and immerse individuals in minutiae instead of creativity. Computer-assisted-planning software, for example, permits you to store data, retrieve a situation analysis of historical information, conduct a spreadsheet analysis of pricing, promotion, or other options, use word processing to facilitate the preparation of the plan, and print out data in a variety of graphic formats. Add-on systems, such as computer modeling, should evolve on an as-needed basis as greater proficiency in planning is demonstrated.

Related to proficiency is the level of knowledge and skills participants need for effective planning. It may be necessary to educate carefully all those who will be involved, from district sales managers to R&D directors. All participants need to understand planning and its outcomes.

5. *Maintain a specific planning schedule.* Line managers, in particular, dislike planning. It takes them away from what they like best, doing action-oriented tasks that produce quick results. To make planning work, however, requires a disciplined approach enforced through firm deadlines. Therefore, to avoid the rushed, panic-oriented approach, allow enough time in the schedule for fact gathering and for a digestive, subconscious approach that allows ideas to be nurtured. Finally, tie in planning to year-round decision making. The management adage "scheduled activities drive out unscheduled activities" applies to the planning activity.

6. *Make strategy and implementation the object of planning.* The written document is not the outcome of the planning activity. It is a "housing" consisting of processes and guidelines for the sole purpose of activating strategies and tactics to be achieved.

You can check the effectiveness of your plan by using these strategy guidelines:

1. *Are there strategies for enlarging current markets?* While a visionary approach in planning is desirable, be certain there are sufficient strategies to enlarge current markets, measured by volume and market share. (This assumes, of course, that maintaining a presence in existing markets remains the planning objective.)

2. *Are there strategies for developing new markets?* A planning imperative, represented by the business portfolio section of the Strategic Marketing Plan, is to penetrate new markets that are emerging, neglected, or poorly served with existing or modified products. Tremendous opportunities are possible for marketing personnel in cooperation with product developers, R&D, and manufacturing people.

3. *Are there clearly defined positions for the company's products?* Two levels of positioning are considered here. The first is the perceptions customers have of your products. For example, you need to know where your customers position your products and company on these scales: high-tech or low-tech; good or poor service; cooperative or unapproachable management; quality or below-industry-standard products. Second, you need to know what position you hold against competitors, as demonstrated by market share, territorial dominance, key account penetration, salesforce strength, technical field support, influence on the channels of distribution, and any other competitive positioning factors considered significant within your industry.

4. *Are there strategies to protect sales volume?* These strategies relate to the quantitative and nonquantitative objectives of the plan. For example, maintaining volume has wide implications, from the internal considerations of keeping a steady flow of products, impacting on production, financial, and support activities, to the external factors of keeping customers' allegiances and keeping competitors from penetrating your customer base.

5. *Are there strategies for launching new products?* If you accept the way marketing defines "new," that is, by the customer's perception, then you have a range of new product alternatives. These include making a minor feature change, designing a major modification, differentiating with value-added services, or developing new-to-the-world products. (In the Business Portfolio box of the Strategic Marketing Plan, these possibilities are listed as new products to existing markets and new products to new markets. Specific actions to launch new products would be detailed in the Strategy section of the plan.)

PART FOUR

Executing the Marketing Presentation

CHAPTER 8

Mobilizing the Marketing Dynamics

The marketing manager has three tasks: to collect and analyze data about the company, the product, and the market; to home in on the precise market and operating environment and try to forecast whatever opportunities and risks lie ahead; and to combine all this information into a solid marketing plan, along with a strategy that will help it succeed.

As we have emphasized in earlier chapters, the marketing plan is a cohesive structure. It is made up of a vast assortment of intelligence, organized in an orderly manner. The plan is designed to reflect company policy and to achieve marketing objectives. It gives the company the information it needs to determine future goals and the focus it should take. In a way, the marketing plan is the vehicle that takes the company from the present into the future.

However, the plan is simply facts and figures; some sort of catalyst is needed to convert it into a strategic model. A plan without strategy is like a group of isolated activities that lack a unifying force. Strategy is the art of coordinating the means (money, manpower, materials) to achieve the end (profit, customer satisfaction, growth) as defined by company policy and objectives.

Companies do not compete against other companies, nor do products compete with products; rather, managements are measured against managements, and strategies compete against strategies. Business is a contest pitting one manager's ability against another's, and the mark of the successful manager is his or her ability not only to select the right facts and figures for a marketing plan but to weld them with the most profitable strategy.

157

Business strategy has its roots in military strategy, and much of what has been developed over the 5,000 years of military history has its parallels in business. The Byzantine general Belisarius, who lived during the first half of the sixth century, said that the most complete and happy victory is to compel one's enemy to give up his purpose, while suffering no harm oneself. Although today's businessman would phrase it differently, achieving such a victory is exactly what a manufacturer wants to do when his or her product's share of the market is threatened and what a shop owner wants to do when faced by competitive pressure from a new discount center in the area.

Whether the strategy is military or business, the goal remains the same—to achieve an objective, as specified by company policy, by employing human and material resources against a variety of obstacles. Developing a marketing strategy requires understanding the environment in which it is formulated and in which it operates and knowing which of these factors can be controlled and which cannot. It also involves recognizing and knowing how to use the characteristics most frequently found in successful strategies; these strategies will be discussed in depth later on in the chapter.

THE STRATEGY'S ENVIRONMENT

Strategy is formulated and carried out in an environment made up of a number of interacting business and social forces. These forces can be divided into two categories—those a company can control and those over which it has little or no control. There are some factors that go beyond the individual manager's control but that the company as a whole can handle; for instance, a sales promotion manager given the job of planning a campaign for a new product probably has no input into the way a product is designed and little control over the funds available for use, but because other members of the staff manage and influence these variables, they can be considered controllable.

Controllable Factors

Controllable factors include:

- Product or service (including all activities involved in design and development)
- Price

- Promotion (including such activities as personal selling, advertising, promotion, and display)
- Distribution (including selecting of distribution channels and means of physical distribution)

These factors—the product or service and the various means used by a company to sell it to a particular market—combine to form what is commonly known as the *marketing mix*. The proper mix of these components in a profitable strategy varies with the needs of the market to be served, the extent of company resources, the general condition of the economy, social and legal considerations, and the nature of the competition. By definition, each element of the marketing mix can be controlled by means of strategy, and each presents a number of challenging variables for the marketing manager.

Product or Service Planning and Development. The actual item for sale, as well as all the activities that go into its development and manufacture, such as type and quality of materials; choice of brand, packaging, and labeling; and degree of standardization are part of the product's involvement in the marketing mix. The product can be a service as well as a tangible item; the company that markets maintenance service is just as concerned with its product as the company that sells furniture.

If a company manufactures the product it sells, it must plan everything—what combination of colors or styles or flavors should be marketed, what shapes and sizes of containers should be used, and what brands and labels should be chosen. Decisions may also involve what services the company should offer in support of its products, what guarantees the products should carry, and under what conditions returns or replacements are to be permitted. If the company is a wholesaler or retailer that buys products from manufacturers, decisions must be made as to which products the company should stock and what services should be offered to back up the product assortment.

Price Determination and Administration. Pricing a product is a challenging part of the marketing mix, even though the final statement in the form of a specific price may appear to be relatively simple. The right price has to take into consideration the competitive products, the structure of the market, and practices in the industry, as well as the condition of the economy.

At the manufacturer's level, pricing considerations include necessary credit terms, warranties, guarantees, and discounts, not to mention production costs and a margin for profit. At the retail level, the pricing decision also takes into account the average markup, markdown, and shrinkage, as well as legal considerations at all levels. The consumer's attitude must also be factored into the price. It is important to remember that customers view price both objectively and subjectively. A price that is just a little too high may turn potential customers away; yet the price should not be so low that even potential new sales will not make enough of a profit. It is a matter of striking the right balance. Manufacturers have to be careful to offer their products in such a way that they return an acceptable profit without turning customers away, and retailers must select product price lines that will attract customers to the store and result in a purchase.

Promotion. The art of promotion encompasses all those activities, both informative and persuasive, that communicate news about products to a selected audience. Sales promotion includes advertising, display, personal selling, publicity, and public relations. (Although public relations is often defined as a nonpromotional activity intended to build and maintain good community relations and a positive company image, the effort automatically has its promotional effect.)

Promotional decisions involve anything from choosing what types of media to advertise in to allocating money for dealer aids or special window displays. Manufacturers direct their promotional efforts both at the dealers who carry their products and at the customers who buy from those dealers. Retailers usually have a single promotional target—that all-important ultimate consumer.

Physical Distribution and Channel Management. The product must be gotten from the manufacturer to the customer for the marketing process to be completed successfully. Historically, physical distribution has been handled on a piecemeal basis, which was grossly inefficient. But advances in transportation and automation and the development of computerized inventory systems are eliminating the bottlenecks. Manufacturers are concerned with the channels of distribution—an organized network of wholesalers, brokers, agents, and retailers that links producers with users—unless they sell directly to the ultimate consumer. All marketers' physical distribution methods are to be used for such areas as traffic and transportation, warehousing, order processing, and some types of inventory control.

Choosing the Marketing Mix. Combining the controllable components of the marketing mix into a successful strategy is the most difficult part of the marketing manager's job. A large enterprise that has many product-price-promotion-distribution combinations can have as many as 5,000 possible marketing mixes from which to develop a strategy. The manager who faces this kind of choice may very well seek an answer in computer simulation models that project and compare the results of various types of strategy in a particular market situation.

However, although the computer is eliminating much of the drudgery connected with working out and comparing the results of taking various kinds of action, the manager must exercise judgment in making the final decision. In spite of all the advances in technology being used, marketing remains just as much an art as a science. Any field that attempts to theorize about people—what they need, what they want, what they will buy—requires a certain degree of intuition to make the leap from one empirical observation to another. The art of determining why people react as they do, to say nothing of how they will react next, is still an uncertain science at best. There is room for instinct and human intuition in determining marketing strategy. Today's educated hunch profits from the information technology can supply.

Uncontrollable Factors

Those elements of the environment that are generally beyond a company's ability to change, modify, or influence are called uncontrollable factors. They include:

- Consumer attitudes and tastes
- Economic conditions
- Legal and social constraints (foreign, federal, state, and local legislation covering trade practices, standards, prices, and exports and imports)
- Available company resources
- The competition

Figure 8-1 depicts the interplay of marketing management variables, which *can* be controlled, with some environmental variables that cannot be. Sometimes a specific industry or product can determine the degree of control—or lack of it—that a company has over one of

Figure 8-1. Elements of marketing management strategy.

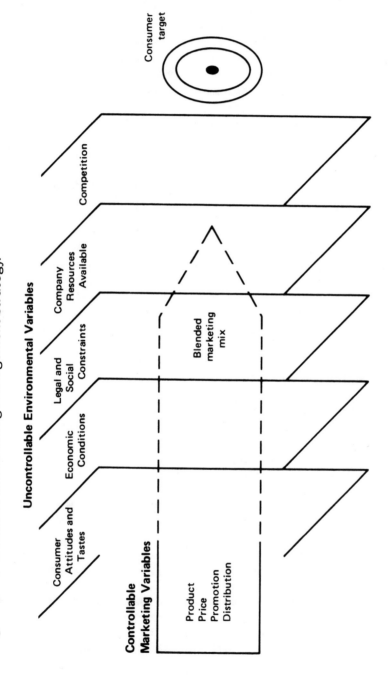

these factors. It is very hard for a company that markets basic construction supplies, such as cement blocks or lumber, to influence consumer attitudes or tastes. Builders already know what they want to handle a specific construction job. On the other hand, a customer in the market for a new car might be swayed by particularly persuasive promotion or attractive price. A customer may start out hunting for a basic family car and end up buying a roomy, sporty minivan.

A company may not be able to control certain conditions that have a significant impact on the company. For example, an organization has little control over the economic conditions within its marketing area, yet the economic situation influences what people buy and how much they are willing to spend. Here are a few of the ways in which uncontrollable factors influence the type of marketing mix a company chooses.

Consumer Attitudes and Tastes. As discussed in Chapter 5, consumers can be divided into different groups or segments according to their attitudes and tastes, the geographic area in which they live, and their average age, income level, educational background, and ethnic heritage. A marketer has to recognize and understand the particular attitudes and life styles of the target group before attempting to serve them properly; although those characteristics cannot be controlled, they determine what the product assortment should contain, what the price levels should be, what services should be offered, even how the outlet should be fixtured and what hours it should be open for business.

For instance, a dress shop in an upper-middle-class, middle-income, suburban neighborhood would probably do best to concentrate on conservative styles at moderate prices, with a sprinkling of extreme styles at higher prices and only an occasional bargain buy. The store should probably be open during normal business hours, including one or two nights a week. Sunday afternoon opening should depend on local custom. The store should have comfortable fixtures and offer a good choice of services, such as credit arrangements and delivery.

A neighborhood delicatessen in an urban area that contains both moderately priced apartment complexes and high-priced cooperative apartment buildings needs different amenities. Its owner need not be too concerned with elaborate fixtures. There should be a wide variety of deli items, delivery service if requested, and the store should be open seven days a week, including evenings.

Economic Conditions. The economic environment of the market in which a company wants to do business is a vital consideration for that company. It is important to realize that the general economy is not the key factor but rather the economic state of the company's potential customers. The relative prices of similar products on the market also play a role.

Marketers who supply all kinds of industrial equipment to steel producers do well when the steel industry is booming. If the federal government cuts back on its contract spending or the automobile industry hints at the possibility of a strike, these suppliers will find their customers very wary about putting money into more equipment. Similarly, in the consumer market, a retailer in a town in which unemployment is a problem and inflation is eating away at the paychecks of those who are employed would be foolish to bring in a new assortment of luxury products. He would do better to concentrate on finding and offering bargains to his customers.

Legal and Social Constraints. In recent years, business has had to grapple with an increasing amount of regulation and social pressure. Legal constraints have been imposed at all levels of government—federal, state, and local—as well as by many foreign countries. Government regulation is carried out in two forms—through laws that must be obeyed as long as they are on the books and through new recommendations made at various levels of government. These recommendations are frequently used by the Federal Trade Commission and the Federal Communications Commission, for example, to suggest what businesses should and should not do. Although not actually law, such recommendations do have government clout behind them, which argues strongly for following them.

These laws and recommendations cover many phases of operating a business, including the methods of competition, prices, taxation, product standards, brands and labeling, and building specifications. As far as the marketer is concerned, it is sometimes helpful to remember that these legal restrictions have two goals: to protect the customer and to protect the marketer against any unfair practices of another marketer.

There have also been vast increases in pressures from various direct and indirect customer groups, limiting or at least requiring a reevaluation of corporate behavior. Examples include pressures for energy-efficient appliances, increased mileage per gallon in cars, pollution- and odor-free facilities, and a reduction in the use of food additives. There are also periodic reactions against sales of particular technologies to certain countries for political reasons; examples in the early 1990s included opposition to trading with Iran, Iraq, China, and Cuba.

Available Company Resources. Planning must be handled within the framework of available company resources—money, manpower, and materials. Managers must know the boundaries of their company's resources in order to work out a realistic plan. A successful marketing effort may very well mean more resources tomorrow, but the manager should not count on using them today.

A company should not plan on trying to market a new product so broadly that it lacks the funds to produce a sufficient quantity of the product to meet demand. Money can be borrowed and equipment and technical skill can be bought, but eventually the loan must be paid back with interest. That purchase is also an investment of present resources, and it must be judged to have a reasonable chance of returning a fair profit on the initial investment.

The Paradox of Competition. Although competition is usually treated as one of the uncontrollable factors in the market environment, there is a paradox in the fact that to change, modify, or influence competition is one of the most important goals of strategic planning. Nevertheless, managers do not have direct control over what the competition does, or who it is. They do not dictate whether competing companies will change their pricing systems, their package designs, or their distribution. However, managers can and do try to alter the marketing situation through personal strategy designed to force the competition to react to their moves.

Competition is one of the key elements of resistance that must be overcome. Elaborate plans are made, products designed, prices determined, advertising worked out, salespeople briefed, distribution channels selected—in fact, the entire organization may shift into high gear simply to outwit the competition. Thus, although an uncontrollable factor in one sense, competition is also one of the prime movers in strategic planning.

Meeting competition head on through the introduction of a new product, entering a new market, or simply attempting to maintain sales volumes of existing products in the face of increasing pressure should never be undertaken lightly or recklessly. A marketing strategy must be worked out that enables the plan to succeed without exhausting valuable company resources.

Before deciding on which strategy to use, a manager must use the facts he or she has collected to weigh the competitive situation in the market. Some markets should be avoided altogether, just as certain products should not even be considered, and certain competitors are best left unchallenged. The manager must be prudent in planning a strategy and yet not be hesitant. The habit of blundering aimlessly into situations should be controlled; on the other hand, if a good opportunity arises, the manager must act swiftly and decisively.

All the aspects of good strategy hang together if the manager is creative and adept. Strategy is an intellectual exercise, a mind-to-mind encounter between managers. The brain waves of strategic confrontation are ultimately transposed into tangible figures in the balance sheets of the competing companies.

THE TWO LEVELS OF STRATEGY

Strategy for the strategic marketing plan is usually worked out on two levels—high-level strategy (or *grand strategy*) and lower-level strategy (or *working strategy*). To some extent, the division is organizational; top management plans and carries out the grand strategy, while middle management is often given the responsibility of planning and carrying out the working strategy.

Grand strategy is the overall plan for the way in which company resources are to be used to achieve company objectives. It works hand in hand with company policy, putting it into action.

Grand strategy takes a long-range view about the company's objectives in the market. A toy company, for example, may have a long-range plan to trade up its product offerings in order to increase the profit per unit without increasing production facilities. Its high-level strategy might specify that the bottom half of the price lines are to be phased out gradually over a period of three years, while new higher-priced items are to be added one by one as resources for their development become available and as testing in the market shows their probable acceptance. Here, the company's grand strategy is designed to take the company's products out of the discount outlets and put them into the higher-priced stores.

Grand strategy is worked out to meet the potential for future development and profitable growth with a minimum expenditure of the company's resources. That toy company does not want to trade up simply by adding new, higher-priced lines, which would require more production expense as well as all the other costs of introducing new products. It intends first to phase out the lower-priced items and then use the freed production time to turn out higher-priced items.

High-level strategy must be developed in accordance with company goals without wasting the company's strength. Depletion of company resources is responsible for more cases of corporate financial exhaustion than is competition. There are numerous cases of companies that have overextended themselves, exhausted their resources, and collapsed, simply because they wanted the immediate satisfaction of winning a market, regardless of the cost and the long-range effect.

The second level of strategy, working strategy, provides a detailed plan that coordinates and activates every facet of the overall marketing plan. The working strategy may be developed by several managers responsible for handling different aspects of the overall plan. The working strategy is continually tested and modified throughout the marketing effort.

Every manager in our toy company example is involved in planning and carrying out a working strategy. The production manager plans how and when to retool the production line for each new product. The sales manager works out new schedules for salespeople that would take them to increasingly higher-priced outlets. The promotion manager thinks up publicity schemes for each new product to underline its better quality.

The success of any strategy depends on sound calculations and careful coordination of the goal and the means to achieve it. The nature of the business world and the problems of predicting customer needs and wants make it difficult for even the most competent manager to make completely accurate calculations, but success is won by the manager whose strategy is based on calculations that come closest to that ideal.

In the sections that follow we take a look at the characteristics most frequently found in successful strategies:

1. Speed
2. The indirect approach
3. Unbalancing the competition
4. Concentrating strength against weakness
5. Alternative objectives

SPEED: THE KEY TO STRATEGY

Perhaps the most important characteristic of any successful planning strategy is the ability to keep the action of the plan moving. Generally, if the action is slow and the company engages in a prolonged, dragged-out marketing effort, it will not be able to withstand the drain on money, manpower, and materials. The result is likely to be failure—not only of the marketing effort, but sometimes of the entire enterprise. What if a competitor comes out with a product or promotional plan similar to the one your company has been struggling with?

A marketing campaign to launch a new product requires considerable work and expenditure of resources at all levels of the organization. The new product needs everything from a package design to warehouse space, and it all has to come out of company resources. To put forth even a modest effort to overcome the typical marketing obstacles and carve out just a small share of the market for the new product will use a sizeable amount of the company's resources before any profit can be realized.

When a sales manager has to budget an appropriation of well over $200 as the average cost of sending a salesperson on a call to a customer or when it costs $100,000 to buy space and design, set up, and run an exhibit booth in a trade show, these expenditures can quickly exhaust the budget. Marketing delays also have a psychological effect. Promotional material that stays around too long begins to lose its impact and effectiveness, and the enthusiasm of the company's sales representatives begins to wane.

The far-reaching effects of speed are demonstrated by the Philadelphia Quartz Company in its product development, long-range planning, and organizational structure, as well as in the actual selling effort. Philadelphia Quartz had the problem of launching a newly developed anti-slip agent, a product that did not fit into the established product line, into the market. It solved the problem by reorganization, making the research and development department responsible to the marketing vice-president (normally, R&D is a separate department). This departmental shift increased the interchange between the people who develop and modify products and those who sell them. By joining the two usually separate functions, the company eliminated six to eight months of the eighteen to twenty-four it normally took to introduce a new product. As a result, the company was able to achieve its ten-year sales projection in less than six years. Considering the long time and high cost of commercializing new products, the speed with which new products are introduced is critical.

While speed is essential to the total marketing strategy, a hasty marketing effort can prove a disaster; on the other hand, there are marketing efforts that turned out successfully in spite of their relatively slow execution. By and large, though, speed pays off. Overlong deliberation, cumbersome committee agendas, long chains of command from the home office to the salespeople in the field, and poor communications all cut down on the speed of action and are detriments to the success of a marketing effort. A marketing effort may lack novelty or ingenuity, but if it is delivered forcefully and at the right point in time, it may well succeed.

In certain industries, accepted practices or traditional buying patterns force speed on marketing plans. An example is the women's ready-to-wear field, in which seasonal changes limit the time available for a plan to succeed. Manufacturers must get their styles accepted and into the stores by the time the season begins or lose most of their sales opportunity. The toy and game field is another example, for many toys and games are fads that have a relatively short selling cycle; marketers who handle these items have to move rapidly to take advantage of the demand.

However, quick action, in the sense discussed here, does not imply recklessness, nor does it condone shoddy products or misleading advertising. It still means a coordinated, well-timed, well-executed plan that moves rapidly to exploit a market opportunity. For that matter, badly made products and false claims used in an attempt to get into the market more quickly probably end up doing more damage to the company than a slight delay would have. No company can afford to sacrifice its standards or indulge in unfair trade practices simply to get the jump on a market demand before a competitor has a chance.

Guidelines for Timing Marketing Efforts

Guidelines for determining how fast a strategy should keep a marketing effort moving and what should be sacrificed for that speed must take company policy and the particular market situation into account. How does a company determine the rate at which a strategy should keep the marketing effort moving and then evaluate whether it is being maintained? There are a number of checks, controls, and measurements a manager can use both to set up a timetable and see whether it is being followed or has bogged down at some point. Much of the information the manager needs is available from the company records; further information can be developed through special market research or can be purchased from outside research sources.

Some useful types of information include:

- *Expense.* Usually prepared on a weekly, monthly, or quarterly basis, these reports list the actual expenditures made during the period, as well as the amount budgeted for the period. The expenditures are usually broken down into categories and then presented as totals and as fractions of the total sales for the same period for further comparison.

- *Sales.* There are many kinds of sales reports. Depending on the company and its recordkeeping requirements, sales figures may be prepared according to time period, geographic area, individual sales representatives, product category, store, department within a store, or by any other category the company finds useful. Actual sales figures for each breakdown are usually shown side by side with the budgeted figures from the marketing plan so the two can be compared to determine if profits are coming in at a sufficient rate to offset expenses.

- *Market share.* Share-of-the-market figures provide a very useful measurement if the total market can be estimated fairly accurately and if the share that the company logically expects to attain can be determined. At specific times during the marketing campaign, the share of the market attained to date can be compared with the goal set for that date. What is most important, however, is that the figures be large enough to be significant. The major automobile manufacturers take share-of-the-market figures very seriously and use them very profitably in planning. On the other hand, a local dress shop would be wasting time if its management were to try to collect and use data on the small share of the garment market it could claim.

- *Warehouse and retail feedback.* Warehouse and retail feedback on product movements produces valuable information about sales and distribution problems. If the product flow stalls at any point—factory, warehouse, wholesaler, or distributor—the feedback will show where the delay is taking place. An interruption in the steady flow of the product could give competitors the time and opportunity to capture additional sales for their products. Product flow should be not only smooth but quick; the speed with which the distribution from manufacturer to the ultimate customer is completed is an important measure of the success of the marketing effort.

- *Product acceptance.* It is not enough to know the product has left the factory or the warehouse. It can sometimes even be misleading to know that it is moving off the marketer's shelves into the hands of the customers. That product might be sitting in the customer's storage room or closet, unused or discarded. The marketer wants to know the degree of customer acceptance of a product, but determining that degree of acceptance is not always easy.

A fair picture of the degree of product acceptance can be drawn by studying customer and dealer reorders. If the product is the type that should be used up quickly, such as soap powder or cereal, then reorders should start coming in very soon if the product has won customer acceptance. For a product that does not bring quick repeat sales, such as a lawn mower or a power drill, dealer reorders indicate that the users have developed confidence in the product. The computer-linked bar code readers and other register scanning systems increasingly in use assist greatly in tracking sales on a dramatically more timely basis.

At the manufacturer's level, a simple telephone survey of dealers and wholesalers sometimes produces valuable feedback about the degree of customer acceptance of a product. If the product is a widely used consumer item, a more extensive survey can be made by telephone and personal interviews.

- *Advertising effectiveness.* Measuring the reaction to advertising can be a key element in determining the progress of a marketing campaign. Most marketing efforts hinge on the effectiveness of the production segment of the plan. People don't beat a path to the door of the company that puts out a better shampoo unless a promotion effort tells them why it is better.

Coupon returns, requests for product information, the degree of store traffic immediately after an ad has appeared, and customer surveys are some of the measures for assessing advertising effectiveness. Although none produces hard and firm figures, each of these checks gives a fair indication of the degree of customer response to advertising and other forms of promotion.

- *The product life cycle.* The concept of the product life cycle is a useful construct for establishing the speed with which a marketing campaign should proceed and for measuring whether the effort is maintaining that speed. All successful products are born, mature, and die. Although each product lives out its own cycle in its own length of time and differs in the length of time it spends at each phase of the cycle, the configuration of the successful product's life takes on a classic pattern of evolution as it advances through the stages of the product life cycle.

More on the Product Life Cycle

The stages of the product life cycle can be viewed by looking at the history of the Jeep Grand Wagoneer, Chrysler's four-wheel drive utility vehicle, which was introduced in the 1960s. It filled a niche in the marketplace for luxury backroad driving. Its sales took off. The unit was seldom offered at reduced price and sold dramatically for more than twenty-five years. Chrysler decided to stop production of the vehicle after 1991 because it was losing market share to newer, strong competition, even though Chrysler did not have a product to replace it; following the logic of the product life cycle, to retain the product would have become increasingly burdensome.

The normal curve for a successful product is illustrated in Figure 8-2. The fundamental concept of the product life cycle is pictured as the classic curve for which the vertical scale measures the sales of the product (also referred to as saturation or customer usage) and the horizontal scale represents the passage of time.

Figure 8-2 plots the life cycle stages of several successful products in the audio electronics industry. The nodes along the normal curve indicate the current approximate position in the life cycle of each product. The offshoots above and below the main curve represent deviations from the typical success story: product failure and product success. The eight-track tape recorder failed before it ever achieved growth when the less cumbersome cassette player was developed, although the product life was extended temporarily when a modified version of the system was produced for use in automobiles. The figure shows the sales for compact discs, or CDs, sweeping up at the right as this new product began to lure customers.

The product life cycle concept is a convenient scheme for classifying products according to stages of acceptance in a particular market. It can be applied to marketing activities such as product planning, forecasting, advertising, and pricing because it provides the framework for grouping products into predictable stages. The process is not a science, however. It is a valuable concept that requires a certain amount of art and judgment in application.

Figure 8-2. The product life cycle for audio electronics products.

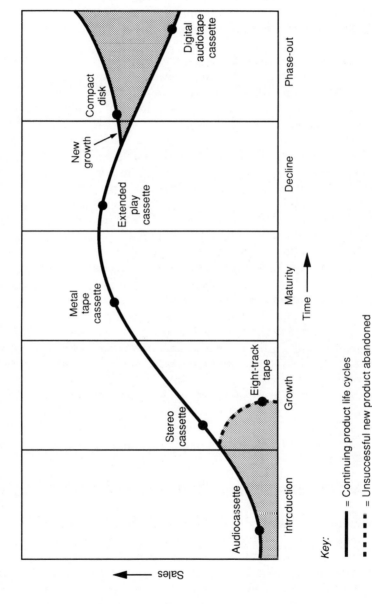

Sales

Introduction Growth Maturity Decline Phase-out

Time →

Audiocassette

Stereo cassette

Eight-track tape

Metal tape cassette

Extended play cassette

New growth

Compact disk

Digital audiotape cassette

Key:

——— = Continuing product life cycles

▪ ▪ ▪ ▪ = Unsuccessful new product abandoned

The marketer who is about to introduce a new product should try to assess what stage of the life cycle similar products are in. It would be foolish, for instance, to introduce a product when similar products are already in the declining phase. If similar products are in the growth phase, then the marketer can logically expect a demand for the product.

Using the product life cycle curve helps the marketer determine how quickly to make a marketing move. The marketer is able to judge how long demand will continue to grow and how long the product will probably stay in its peak phase by determining the phase that similar products are in.

Once the campaign is under way, the marketing manager can judge the product's prospects for success by the shape of its life cycle. If the typical growth pattern does not develop, the marketer might be wise to reevaluate the marketing strategy. A product that isn't going to make it should be withdrawn from the market before it hurts profits or reputation significantly. This occurs with surprising regularity in the auto industry. Often a new automobile is introduced with much investment and promotion but simply does not develop a healthy sales pattern, one that reflects the normal life cycle of a successful product. The company finally abandons the effort completely, feeling that any further expenditure would be wasted.

Sometimes the marketing effort can be saved by a change in strategy. The company has to reanalyze the various elements in the marketing mix and put them together in a new way to formulate a different strategy. Once a strategy has failed, however, it should never be repeated, even if it seems to have better application to another marketing situation, because the strategy has already been seen by the competition, which will have had time to develop even better ways to defeat it.

Product strategies are discussed in greater detail in Chapter 9.

MARKETING USING THE INDIRECT APPROACH

In addition to speed, a second characteristic of successful marketing strategies is the use of an indirect approach in overcoming whatever obstacles stand in the way of the marketing plan's success. An indirect approach means taking a different path toward the desired goal, making a move that confuses the competition and masks the real goal the marketer is seeking. Such an approach is used to throw the competition off balance, not only psychologically but sometimes even physically. The indirect approach is like an end run in football; the goal is directly ahead, but the ball carrier runs off at an angle, avoiding a head-on attack on the line and using indirection to baffle the opposing team and gain some yardage in his fight toward the goal.

A classic example of using an indirect approach, valuable for its clarity, is that of L'EGGS, a division of Hanes Corporation, which opened a new distribution channel for pantyhose and stockings. Prior to the market entry of L'EGGS, the main line of distribution for the "big three" companies—Burlington, Kayser-Roth, and Hanes—was through department stores and specialty shops. Hanes's strategy was to take an indirect approach, to bypass its competition and enter a new distribution channel—supermarkets and drugstores. The company created a brand name, L'EGGS, used a unique package in the shape of an egg, and set up an attractive display rack. It also set up a network of "route girls" to service the racks.

Hanes went even further when it took the unorthodox approach of asking the store managers to allow two-and-one-half square feet of space for the display and to take the hosiery on consignment. The practice of consignment selling was generally avoided by other merchandise sellers, specifically the inexpensive foreign hosiery brands, because it does not require an investment or risk on the part of the store manager. Two years after the marketing effort for L'EGGS was launched, it was selling 74 percent of the major urban markets in the United States and had achieved first place as the largest-selling brand of hosiery in supermarkets and drugstores, with sales of $35 million.

The Profits Reaped by Unorthodoxy

The indirect approach is part of that valuable planning device—unorthodoxy. Unorthodox thinking defies the traditional way of doing things, the rigid thinking, the set rules, the by-the-book approach. It represents a new twist and depends on originality and surprise to achieve success. Enterprises that have violated the traditional ways of making marketing moves and used the indirect approach have proved how well such methods work.

For many years marketers of phonograph records, tapes, and CDs felt the need to use retail outlets in order to sell their products, partly because of an earlier practice of having listening rooms for customers to hear the selections prior to purchase. Not true, said some unorthodox companies led by Columbia Record Club, now Columbia

House—which proceeded to prove its point by selling millions of records, audio tapes, CDs, and videotapes through the mail.

For a long time, pharmaceutical houses operated under the assumption that proprietary drugs could be sold successfully only through drugstores. A few companies challenged that idea, and now a number of drugs are sold successfully in all kinds of outlets, including supermarkets and through the mail. One market that had seemed impenetrable was the soft drink market, dominated by giants such as Coca-Cola, Canada Dry, and Pepsi Cola. Schweppes managed to find a weak spot in one segment—ginger ale and tonic water—used a lively promotional campaign as a wedge, and won itself a narrow, but profitable, share of the business.

Another example is the auto industry. Detroit was sure that small cars were just a fad during the 1960s and early 1970s and made little effort to reach the market for low-priced, fuel-efficient imported cars. As a result, dozens of brands of foreign cars, with names entirely new to U.S. consumers, were able to gain effective entry into the domestic market. They kept their prices competitively low by ignoring the Detroit tradition that car styling had to change every year. The result has been a continuing and probable future shift in market share from Detroit, which had until that time been one of the envies of international corporate life, to overseas car makers.

In another case, Sony entered the U.S. electronics market not by tackling such giants as RCA, Westinghouse, and General Electric head on but by using the indirect approach and carving out a profitable piece of the market through the development of miniature TVs, personal radios, and similar new products.

The Problem With a Direct Approach

Strategy based on a direct approach, on doing the expected, often makes a company particularly vulnerable to the competition. The direct approach usually means using standard tactics and well-known ideas and copying current fads in advertising themes or product design. Doing the predictable often results in a marketing effort that looks dull and too "me-too-ish" to prospective customers. It gives the competition an opportunity to woo customers with a more interesting approach.

Managers who insist on using direct methods are usually overly concerned with making mistakes that might be held against them. They don't want to take chances, so they use the traditional tactics, the obvious strategy; as a result, of course, their marketing moves are obvious to the competition. Direct methods simply don't pay off.

The unexpected approach baffles the competition, which may react by making mistakes that translate into opportunities for the challenging company. In most cases, an indirect approach throws the competition off course only temporarily, but even a brief upset may be long enough to give the company the chance it needs to prepare for the next move. The diversion seldom lasts long enough to eliminate the competition altogether from the market, but it is highly unlikely that a marketing effort would be directed toward such a goal anyway; few companies have the resources required for such an effort, and any marketing company that even seems to be attempting to monopolize a market soon finds itself in the federal courts.

UNBALANCING THE COMPETITION

A third characteristic of successful strategies in marketing plans is the use of any move that puts the competition off balance and thus weakens its reactions to the developing marketing campaign. Like a multiple offense in football, the goal of such a move is to cut down the effectiveness of the competition's response by spreading it out as thinly as possible, by diverting and confusing it.

The move to "unbalance" the competition may be the most important piece of strategy in the entire marketing plan. This is the move that forces the competition to react defensively and *change*. Remember the paradox of competition? Competition is usually listed as an uncontrollable factor; yet to make the competition change is the goal of most marketing efforts. Despite this, an effort to put the competition off balance, as with all other moves in strategy, must be done with the lowest possible expenditure of company resources. A manager must never forget that the extent to which any marketing plan is successful is measured in the financial terms of net profit or return on invested capital.

Types of Moves

A move that causes the competition to reassess its situation can involve physical or psychological action, often a combination of the two. If the competition is successfully holding onto an important share of a market or is making a strong bid for a bigger piece, it must be because that competition has found the right marketing mix. If a marketer can cause an imbalance in that marketing mix in any way whatsoever, it is likely that the competition's reactions and market position will be weakened.

The Physical Maneuver. A physical move to weaken the competition's position usually takes into consideration the market conditions, the marketing mix of both companies, and some careful timing. Based on the conditions of the market, the maneuver usually involves shifting some physical resources at a time and in a way calculated to force the competition into making a quick countermove.

For instance, a company might have a marketing objective of increasing its share of a particular two-state market area from 12 percent of the total sales made to 18 percent. Standing in the way of that objective, however, is a strong competitor that seems perfectly capable of holding onto its share of the market. The company's strategy, therefore, might include an attempt to change the market situation by focusing a maximum sales promotion campaign on those two states, using increased advertising and shifting additional salespeople from other territories. In addition, the company might set up improved facilities in the area for fast production and distribution to assure dealers of plentiful supplies and quick delivery of reorders.

Even though these moves would be obvious in their intent, they would still be able to change the marketing situation. The competition would then be forced to change its marketing mix to meet the challenge. For instance, a competitive manager might also step up the advertising campaign. This move would represent a switch from what had been a successful marketing mix for the competition—a change in the balance of product, price, promotion, and distribution.

The Psychological Maneuver. Psychology plays its part, too, in unbalancing the competition. Often a manager makes a marketing move that may not directly challenge the competition but is intended to make the competition uneasy and unsure. A series of teaser ads saying "Wait until you see what we've got for you in September" can start the competition wondering whether the innovation is going to be a new product, an improvement or change in a standard product, or a change in price. Again, the move, although only psychological, has its unsettling, disconcerting effect.

The action of L'EGGS to circumvent its major competitors and gain a major marketing share through supermarkets and drugstores had an unbalancing psychological effect on its competitors' managers. In addition, it would be reasonable to assume that the marketing managers of the low-priced overseas brands of hosiery already in supermarkets felt the unbalancing effect of the fast-moving, innovative, and indirect approach of the L'EGGS strategy.

The Decision

The deciding factor in knowing what move will most disconcert the competition is understanding just where and how the competition is vulnerable, what is needed to take advantage of that vulnerability, and whether the results are likely to be worth the cost. The purpose of the strategy is to get the competition to react in some way other than through its traditional strength. The hope is that the competition will spread out its resources and disrupt its marketing mix, thus changing its marketing strategy. Even if the strategy of unbalancing the competition does not in itself achieve the final objective of the marketing effort, it does confuse the competition and prepare the way for future attainment of that objective.

One example of a company's unbalancing its major competitors in an intensely competitive market is that of computer giant IBM. IBM uses its computer maintenance business as an unbalancing advantage over competitors such as Digital Equipment, Compaq, Apple, and Toshiba. However, implementing the strategy is more complicated than simply promoting a maintenance service.

Some market background: Maintenance fees during 1988–1989 plummeted in the computer industry as a result of the improved quality of computers and a reduction in the maintenance required (reliability averages 99.5 percent) and the ability of smaller machines to do the work once done by computer mainframes, making replacement frequently easier than repair. Whereas in the past 10 percent of equipment costs had been set aside for maintenance, that figure fell to only 4 percent.

How then does IBM create an unbalancing effect over its competitors with maintenance service?

- IBM uses maintenance to win back many customers who had defected to the competition by servicing all equipment, not just IBM equipment.
- IBM sells contracts for maintenance and related services, leading to a profitable computer replacement business.

- IBM service personnel constantly visit customer locations, providing an early warning system for impending big-ticket purchases.
- IBM establishes effective relationships for basic maintenance, leading to sales of more elaborate services, such as designing and building data centers, planning networks, and even operating entire computer departments.

According to an industry executive, "These new areas are growing in the high double digits or better." Fixing broken equipment is expected to be only a minor part of a computer maker's service business.

For IBM, maintenance and technical services have evolved into a potent marketing weapon that has an unbalancing effect on competition. Specifically, the service supports IBM's promotional efforts with precise intelligence about customers' intentions, develops a physical presence on customers' premises, and provides total solutions for customers' problems with added services, thereby increasing the value of the order.

The Marketing Center of Gravity

When attempting to unbalance the competition, the important element to look for and isolate, in both the competition's marketing mix and the company's own marketing mix, is what's called the *marketing center of gravity*. The marketing center of gravity, or MCG, is the pivot in any company's marketing mix, the strength on which everything else depends.

The MCG can be used in any area of the marketing mix. It can be the product itself or the advertising that the company uses. It can be the personal selling techniques developed by the company or the type of distribution outlets it uses. Every company's marketing mix has its own particular strong point, its own focus of strength, its own MCG on which the company's success depends. To locate and study a company's MCG, a manager needs:

- A *market information system* that supplies regular, continuing, up-to-date data about the market and the companies competing in the market. The information supplied should be complete enough to allow a manager to anticipate problems, identify opportunities, and prepare a marketing strategy.

- *An organizational structure* with rapid lines of communication between the people in the field and the decision makers in the home office, a communications network that cuts through all the layers of management to get the needed information to the right people as quickly as possible.

Finding out exactly what a competitor's MCG is helps the company shape the plans that can unbalance the competitor's position. What the company wants to do is to reduce the effectiveness of the pivotal point, that MCG, so that all the other parts of the marketing effort will be less effective as well. The MCG can be made less effective by matching marketing mixes or emphasizing different mixes, depending on which tactic a manager thinks will be most successful without increasing costs. In the IBM example, the company decided that one of its strengths—service—matched a weakness in the rest of the industry. IBM decided to take advantage of this situation and aggressively use its maintenance services to unbalance its competitors and shift the marketing center of gravity to its advantage.

CONCENTRATING STRENGTH AGAINST WEAKNESS

The fourth characteristic of a successful marketing strategy is also the next logical move—a concentration of a company's strongest resources on selected segments of markets and at the weakest point in the competition's marketing mix.

A concentration of resources means focusing money, staff resources, and materials on segments of the market where there is an identified need for a product or service. It also means concentrating resources where there are one or more weaknesses in the competitor's marketing capabilities; for example, there might be some deficiency in the product, inadequate distribution and service, ineffective promotion to move prospects to the point of purchase, or an inability to price the product or service to gain a major share of the market.

The mark of a successful marketing manager is the ability to judge his or her own company's marketing resources and then to compare its strengths and weaknesses against those of the competitor—to determine whether it is wise to enter a market as measured against the accepted standards of sales, profits, and return on invested capital.

Sometimes a weakness in the competition's marketing mix is obvious at the beginning of the marketing effort, and the manager's preliminary moves are made simply to increase this weakness. The marketing manager at L'EGGS, for example, saw that even though the competing foreign hosiery brands were low-priced, they had vulnerabilities—they were of low quality, the brand names were not nationally advertised, the packaging and display lacked excitement and eye appeal, they required an up-front financial investment in inventory from the store manager, and, above all, they did not fill the void that existed at the time of Hanes's entry into supermarkets and drugstores. Thus, two situations existed for a concentrated marketing effort. First, there was an identified need for quality, brand-name hosiery conveniently available through supermarkets and drugstores; second, there were weaknesses in the competitors' marketing efforts.

Unless a company has a monopoly in the production of a product or in its distribution, both of which are unlikely in the normal marketplace, it cannot fill all the distribution channels or reach all the potential customers. Therefore, it must have weaknesses somewhere, which means opportunities always exist. Weaknesses can be found almost anywhere in the marketing mix, and opportunities can arise almost anywhere in the marketplace. It could be a poorly trained and ineptly managed selling staff, a lack of proper quality checking on the production line, or ineffectual advertising; perhaps the company has exhausted itself financially. Any one of these conditions constitutes a major weakness that can be exploited by the right kind of marketing strategy.

A few years ago, Philip Morris, Inc., sensed that it was not using its field force as effectively as it might. To substantiate that hunch, it launched a massive computerized study covering every retail outlet in the country, from giant supermarket chains down to the corner mom-and-pop store. With this huge mass of data, Philip Morris isolated the high-volume outlets that required four or more calls a month. Then came the medium-volume outlets that might need one or two calls a month. Finally, there were the low-volume retailers, which might not be called on more than once or twice a year, during special sales drives. At that point, the company plotted the location of the outlets and reassigned its work force to concentrate on points of high sales and maximum profit opportunity. Prior to the study, there might have been three people in North Dakota and three in San Francisco, whereas the best concentration of selling power required only one in North Dakota and four in San Francisco, leaving an additional person available for troubleshooting or for staff reduction.

The application of concentration was part of Philip Morris's strategy. By examining the number and location of warehouses, Philip Morris was able to consolidate and concentrate a warehouse network that achieved overnight product delivery to sales outlets. Like all other characteristics of good strategy, the strategy of concentrating strength against opportunity is more of an intellectual device than a physical encounter. It is not only a matter of which company has the better sales staff, the bigger ad budget, or the larger manufacturing capabilities; it is also a question of how and when a company effectively maneuvers these resources in the marketing effort.

Shape of the Market

If strengths are recorded as peaks on a chart and weaknesses are recorded as valleys, then a company's marketing mix takes on a definite shape. The prudent manager bases a marketing strategy on what he or she finds to be the "shape" of the competition and on how the shape of the markets is plotted. The various information systems, whether from informal sales reports from representatives in the field or from formal market research, give the manager the detailed information needed to determine the shape of the competition's marketing mix as well as have an up-to-date picture of any changes in the market. Philip Morris's study helped the company determine the shape of the marketplace and how to allocate resources to conform to that shape.

Only when a company has manipulated its competition can it know the best point to concentrate on—what point would be the least likely to withstand a concentrated effort against it. However, managers want to keep the competition from doing exactly the same thing to their companies; they want to disguise their marketing plans and strategy.

When preparing for a concentrated effort, good strategy often includes preliminary moves. For example, a manufacturer prepared for a concentrated effort in a particular geographic area might introduce a new product in another area simply to mislead the opposition. The distraction might well draw some of the competition's strength away from the market area and increase the chance of success for a concentrated effort. A small company with limited financial, production, and marketing resources might wait for the industry leaders to bring out a new product. If it becomes a success, the small company can then turn out a version of it and hunt for a piece of the market. To get that chunk will take clever strategy—but the small company will have saved its resources, having spent little, if any, in developing and testing the product idea and will have learned a good deal about the marketing mix of the successful larger company.

In another version of this strategy, a small company might indicate, through deliberate information leaks and promotional activity, that it intends to market a new product. This might lead a major company to react by trying to get a similar product onto the market first. This gives the smaller company the opportunity to check the profitability and consumer acceptance of such a product and to study the marketing mix of the larger company.

The success of the strategy of concentration of resources usually depends on a definite plan for thinning out or weakening the competition's strength before the effort takes place, as well as examining the shape of the market. Shaping the competition shows a company exactly where the competition is weakest and where the opportunities are the greatest.

Cumulative Concentration

Although the concentration of resources against the competition and market segments is one of the key elements of a successful strategy, it can also be a dangerous technique unless it is thoroughly understood and carefully used. Simply harnessing all the available money, staff resources, and materials against one point is not going to succeed unless the competition is unable to defend itself at that point. The wise manager commits his or her company to such a course of action and uses its strength only when the situation ensures a good chance of success.

Sometimes success requires a cumulative action rather than a single effort. The concentration of a marketing effort does not necessarily mean taking all the resources and applying them with one tremendous thud against one point of the competition's marketing mix. It does not mean, for instance, that the entire budget should be sunk into one promotional effort nor that one product should be relied on to carry the entire weight of achieving the marketing objectives.

Instead, a concentrated effort should be launched. A single ad, a single salesperson, or a single product improvement is not enough to make the marketing effort succeed. The effort usually combines the company's strongest assets in a series of cumulative programs. For instance, a single ad in a trade magazine may cause a purchasing manager to remember the product for a few days. An ad followed up by a sales letter may keep the product in the purchasing manager's mind for a few weeks. An ad followed up by a sales letter and then a call by a salesperson will probably fix the product firmly in the mind of the purchasing manager and may result in a sale.

ALTERNATIVE OBJECTIVES

The final characteristic found in successful strategies is the existence of alternative objectives. These should both be sequential and involve alternatives. In other words, the strategy should contain a series of objectives to be attained, one after another, and there should be alternative objectives at each step.

Alternative objectives give the plan flexibility and allow a company to react to changes without losing any headway toward the marketing effort's ultimate goal. If a plan has but a single objective that proves impossible to reach, the entire marketing effort has to be written off as worthless. If the plan has a series of alternative objectives, the company has a good chance of obtaining at least one objective and using that success as a stepping-stone toward the next step.

Alternative objectives also help confuse the competition. If the company has only one objective, the competition will probably learn what it is and use all its strength to defeat the marketing effort. If, on the other hand, the company has a series of alternative objectives, the competition won't know which area to defend. No matter how competing defenses are moved, the company will always be able to switch its marketing effort to an alternative objective.

Put in practical terms, it is the case of the hardware store owner who wanted to get some of the construction hardware business but wasn't sure of what kind of supplies to handle. What the management wanted was an increase in sales volume through the development of a specialty product line. After studying the market, the owner developed a strategy involving a choice of objectives that could be reached either by adding a comprehensive line of plumbing hardware or by adding a full line of interior fixtures.

First, the store brought in and promoted a relatively modest stock of both plumbing hardware and interior fixtures. Volume gradually increased, and it became clear that most of the increase was in the plumbing hardware. A study of the total sales figures and the marketing situation showed that most of the interior fixtures business was still going to a firmly entrenched local company, but that none of the other companies offering plumbing hardware had built up any particularly strong hold on their customers. The hardware store then dropped its line of interior fixtures, concentrated on plumbing hardware, and achieved its goal of developing a profitable specialty.

TWO ZONES OF ACTIVITY

A company's marketing plan strategy involves winning more business, usually by combatting competition in a particular market. It is equally important, however, that a company's strategy take into consideration the wants and the needs of the customer in terms of both today's and tomorrow's environment. As the social, political, and economic environment changes, so does the customer. In the end, satisfying the customer is the reason the marketer stays in business. These, then, are the two zones of strategy activity that the manager must balance: the competition and the customer.

The Competition

Making a marketing plan and formulating its strategy to defend or develop a market requires decisiveness, resoluteness, and firmness. The keys to success in formulating a strategy can be summed up as follows:

- First, adjust the objectives to the available resources. In determining a marketing objective, calculate what is possible to achieve. Do not take on more than the company logically can handle. Work with the full realization that, as the marketing effort develops, unexpected situations that will take more of the resources than originally planned will also develop. Therefore, don't figure too close to the limits of available personnel, money, and materials in any effort, and don't plan a marketing effort that involves an unrealistic and probably unattainable objective.

- Second, keep the objectives in mind at all times. Adapt the plan to the circumstances, realizing that there is more than one way to achieve each objective. The plan should be flexible—and every action should take the company a little closer to the final objective.

- Third, choose a course that the competition does not expect. Try to determine a course that will surprise the competition and catch it off guard as well as take the company closer to the final objective, for that course will be the one that the competition will find hardest to defeat.

- Fourth, take the line of least resistance. Don't batter against the competition's strongest point. Concentrate instead on a weakness in its marketing mix, just as long as the action contributes to the movement toward the ultimate market objectives and the company can use its strength efficiently.

- Fifth, develop a plan that includes alternative objectives. By putting the competitor in the position of not being sure what kind of marketing effort to expect, the company has the chance of gaining at least one objective and may be able to use that success to reach for the next. But don't confuse the value of establishing a single, coordinated marketing plan, which is a must, with picking only a single objective, which is dangerous.

- Sixth, don't repeat a plan or strategy in its same form if it fails. Simply adding more resources to an unsuccessful strategy will not bring success. Not only will the competition know what form the marketing effort will take, but the time it takes to reinforce the effort will give the competition time to strengthen its defenses.

Finally, keep these tips in mind:

- The more strength a manager wastes when entering a market, the greater the risk that the competition will be able to defeat the marketing plan. Even if a manager eventually succeeds in winning the market, a large part of the possible profits will have been eaten up in the process.

- Although the tools of the marketing mix are physical (product, price, promotion, and distribution), putting them together into a marketing mix is a mental process. The better the strategy, the more likely it is to gain the objectives of the marketing plan and the less that victory is likely to cost.

- The closer to the line between what is ethical and what is nonethical a manager's marketing practices are, the more bitter the competition will be, hardening the very resistance the manager is trying to overcome.

- If the contest for a share of the market is going to be too costly, the manager should abandon it or rework the strategy to bring the ratio of cost and profit into line.

The essential sequence in establishing a marketing strategy for a marketing effort is first to create the opportunity, and then to exploit it. A company cannot enter a market or hold onto its share of a market unless it first creates the opportunity to do so. It cannot succeed in its objectives unless it then exploits that opportunity. In other words, success doesn't just happen; it is planned.

One final comment about the competition: Remember, a marketing manager has to take into consideration the need to learn to live with the competition and protect the profits that the market is providing for every company in it. Excessive discounting and price wars don't really change the market for the customer, but they do eliminate the chance for an adequate profit margin for all companies involved.

The Customer

Marketing plan strategy should always relate the product to the customer and the environment in which the customer lives. Marketing objectives go far beyond profits and sales. They must involve more than merely satisfying today's customer and doing so at a profit. The goals must also take into consideration what tomorrow's customer is going to want and how tomorrow's environment will affect the decisions of that customer.

A company has both an involvement in and a commitment to the environment in which its customers live, for environmental changes shape market changes. First, environmental changes can cause problems in what have been established and profitable markets. For instance, companies that make cigarettes are facing increasing promotion restrictions and increasing social disapproval because the product they offer has been proved to be detrimental to people's health. Companies that manufacture firearms for civilian use are facing almost constant demand for federal and state legislation that would not only sharply restrict their marketing activities but might put many of them out of business. Even toy companies are having their problems, for various groups are demanding that toys be safer for children. New requirements on toy manufacturers, for instance, require that toys be made so small parts can not break or fall off to be swallowed by young children and that the corners on toys not be sharp or jagged.

Reflecting concerns of health and safety, eating habits have changed so markedly during the past decade that products with many years of successful sales find themselves having difficult times. Although technically these companies are practicing the marketing concept by producing and selling a product that satisfies a specific group of customers, a change in the environment is putting steadily increasing pressure on them that may eventually change the entire market picture.

At the same time, environmental changes are creating new opportunities. For instance, some toy companies have put out lines of multiethnic toys, such as dolls with black features and Afro hairstyles, and have discovered that these lines have not only met demands for social responsibility but have increased sales as well. Other companies are developing and marketing products and services to handle some of the major concerns of the day—for example, new ways to treat illness, to build low-rent housing, and to cut down air pollution and water pollution. As one marketing expert has said, "One of the next marketing frontiers may well be related to markets that extend beyond mere profit considerations to intrinsic values, to markets based on social concern, markets of the mind, markets concerned with the development of people to the fullest extent of their capabilities." Good strategy will be the essential catalyst for plans concerning these new markets.

CHAPTER 9

Solving Marketing Problems: A Practical Guide to Selecting Marketing Strategies

Peter F. Drucker, the well-known management educator, author, and consultant, has stated, "The object of business is to create a customer."[1] Expanding on that thought, an additional object of business is to create and maintain a thriving and growing marketplace. Both objects are achieved through strategy. Strategy, in this context, as discussed in the previous chapter, is the art of coordinating the means (money, human resources, materials) to achieve the end (profit, customer satisfaction, company growth) as defined by company policy and objectives.

However, achieving these admirable goals is difficult in a volatile environment of conflicting forces embracing industry, customer, and competitive changes. Each has the potential to create barriers that prevent the company from realizing those noble ideals. The conflicting forces pose problems—*marketing problems*—that need solutions by means of strategy. Some major problems faced by large and small companies in the 1990s are these:

1. *The Practice of Management* (New York: Harper & Row, 1954), pp. 37–38.

- How to outperform the industry in a mature market
- How to effectively position products against market leaders
- How to become a niche market leader
- How to differentiate a commodity product and reduce the pressure on price

Let's examine each problem and see marketing strategy in action.

CASE EXAMPLE FOR MARKETING PROBLEM 1: HOW DO YOU OUTPERFORM THE INDUSTRY IN A MATURE MARKET?

Owens-Corning Fiberglass Corporation faced tough times as a producer of fiberglass insulation and fiberglass-reinforced plastic in a mature market. Its core product line, the famous pink insulation for the building industry, had been sliding for three years. Also, its plastics operation had suffered with the decline in car and boat sales. To compound the problem, the economy entered a recession. Clearly, Owens-Corning was operating within a total industry-depressed economy. Owens-Corning used several tactics to counter the problem.

Let's examine Owens-Corning's strategies:

- In what appears to be an obvious action, Owens-Corning cut costs. This was not indiscriminate cutting, however, but savings achieved with a strategic vision toward chasing opportunities after the recession. All levels of managers probed for ways to maintain a strengthened position through more efficient operations, readying the company to sprint ahead of competitors at the proper time. In four years, managers saved $200 million in production costs alone.

- Managers relentlessly searched for new market opportunities. To reduce exposure to the depressed construction market, they refocused objectives on fiberglass industrial plastics with new applications.

- Product developers created new products from existing materials and technologies. For example, fancy new designs of fiberglass roof shingles were developed; new insulation with extra protection was introduced. (In the latter example, the improved insulation took advantage of the rise in heating oil for residential and industrial structures.)

- Marketing and technical personnel, working with fiberglass customers worldwide, initiated new uses for Owens-Corning's materials. Peugeot, for example, agreed to use fiberglass-reinforced plastic in the front end of one of its car models.

Guide to Marketing Strategy

Managing in a recessionary environment requires a delicate balance between people and activities, regardless of your level in the organization.

Consider the critical people/activity balance of the following actions: cutting costs and people to maintain profitability, ensuring that personnel preserve product quality, maintaining customer satisfaction through product performance, and providing ongoing technical and customer-service assistance.

Then, what about managerial attitudes during the recessionary period? Outwardly, you must continue motivating your staff even while you are immersed in cost-chopping and people-cutting, encouraging them to introduce new products, pushing them to find methods of adding value to existing products, and searching for techniques to safeguard a viable competitive position. Finally, you must prepare for the postrecession period by planning how to go after those opportunities shelved during the down period.

The above strategies apply not only to large organizations but especially to mid-size and smaller organizations that are even more vulnerable to the shock waves of recession.

Implementing strategies to outperform the industry in a mature market depends on leadership and managerial capabilities. Consider the following leadership factors:

1. *Global perspective.* Try to think strategically with a total business perspective, not just a product focus. Hard as it may be when you are scratching for sales, look to new market opportunities. Also, watch for the surprise entry of new global competitors that are looking for additional sales by targeting *your* customers.

2. *Entrepreneurial thinking.* As in Owens-Corning's case, look for new product applications, neglected market niches, ways to redesign old products or add value to them, and new approaches to building relationships with customers for specific applications to solve their problems.

3. *Planning capability.* Whether it is simple or complex, insist on

maintaining a formal planning system. The planning document solid-
ifies ideas, serves as a communications vehicle, and provides guidelines to keep you and others on track.

4. *Team approach.* Involve managers from every functional area of
the business. Pull them together for the common goal of survival and
growth. Dedicate a team to *each* major market segment or product
line, and, if possible, *empower* it with the authority to make decisions.

5. *Implementation.* The ability to develop plans is but one part of
the equation. The second part is implementation. Follow up; be sure
action is taken.

CASE EXAMPLE FOR MARKETING PROBLEM 2: HOW DO YOU EFFECTIVELY POSITION YOUR PRODUCTS AGAINST MARKET LEADERS?

A. Schulman, Inc., produces plastics that go into such diverse products as auto dashboards, moldings, and furniture. The company produced extraordinary results during a five-year period ending in 1990
by doubling sales and tripling earnings. Its performance triumphed
in a competitive environment against such mighty companies as Dow
Chemical, Monsanto, BASF, and Hoechst.

Let's examine the key success strategies:

- Schulman excelled in filling rush orders for customers by making special weekend runs in its U.S. and European factories to satisfy
customers' urgent requests.

- Schulman talked quality and product differentiation—not
price. While the industry giants focused heavily on commodity plastics, Schulman positioned itself with higher-priced specialty products.
Managers searched for areas of differentiation with features that
couldn't be duplicated easily by competitors.

- In its early years of growth, Schulman established strong customer relationships with smaller organizations— those that were generally neglected by the market leaders. Then, by using superior technology to add value to product offerings and by continuing its
customer-driven relationships, it expanded to serve such names as
General Motors, Ford, and 3M.

- Commitment to a market-driven attitude became a hard-and-fast policy at Schulman. Its labs did not develop compounds and then search for markets. Rather, salespeople and engineers worked closely with customers on ideas that solved problems. Those ideas were then converted into customized products to provide solutions.

▪ About 65 percent of Schulman's sales are outside the United States. Beyond its presence in Canada, the United Kingdom, and Europe, the Akron, Ohio, company cultivated thriving relationships with Japanese companies, such as Mitsubishi. The alliance provided unique opportunities to supply auto moldings and dashboards for Toyota and Honda plants in the United States.

Guide to Marketing Strategy

If you want to position your product effectively against market leaders, consider some of the following action strategies suggested by the Schulman case:

1. *Select a competitive advantage that larger competitors cannot perform efficiently.* Employ market research, such as customer-tracking studies, to identify possibilities for differentiation.

2. *Commit to quality and service as an organizational priority.* Initiate programs that encourage individuals at various functions to strive for quality. These are not one-time motivational talks but involve continuous training.

3. *Focus on specialty products that command premium prices; leave the commodity price segment to others.* Practice segmenting your market for specific product applications. Get closer to your customers—and their problems.

4. *Establish long-term alliances with customers to grow with them and to build technology and product relationships.* Encourage trusting relationships with customers or suppliers so that sensitive information can be shared for mutual interests.

5. *Maintain a market-driven orientation throughout the organization—within all functions—to maintain a competitive edge.* Organize strategy teams made up of multifunctional managers. Then use the teams' strategic marketing plans as communication linkages with field sales in order to respond rapidly to market opportunities.

6. *Seek global opportunities that represent long-term objectives.* Through joint ventures, licensing, or exporting, develop a global

presence (if international markets are consistent with the corporate mission).

7. *Partner salespeople with customers to provide product solutions to customer problems.* Go beyond traditional forms of sales training. Instead, teach salespeople how to *think* like strategists so they can help their customers achieve competitive advantage.

8. *Identify market niches that are emerging, neglected, or poorly served.* Reassess how you currently segment your markets. Search for additional approaches beyond the usual criteria of customer size, frequency of purchase, or geographic location. Look for potential niches by clustering groups of prospective buyers by just-in-time delivery, product performance, application, quality, or technical assistance.

CASE EXAMPLE FOR MARKETING PROBLEM 3: HOW DO YOU BECOME A NICHE MARKET LEADER?

Tandy Corporation, as well as its consumer electronics chain of Radio Shack stores, is positioned favorably as a niche leader in terms of sales and profit margins when compared to large retailers such as Circuit City, Businessland, Highland Superstores, and MicroAge. And as a computer manufacturer, Tandy ranks a respectable third in sales behind IBM and Apple and is slightly ahead of IBM on net return on sales. Even with an allegedly stuffy image (some consumers don't equate Tandy and Radio Shack with high technology), the Fort Worth, Texas, company sells over $1 billion of its computers a year.

Its quality image to the trade is so high that Digital Equipment Corporation and Matsushita, among others, are buying Tandy-produced computers to sell under their own names. The notebook and desktop computer models that Tandy makes for Matsushita's Panasonic line are sold in computer stores nationwide. In still another successful customer relationship, N. V. Philips of Holland agreed to have Tandy build an innovative tape deck, designed to play both digital and conventional audiocassettes.

One of the exceptional aspects of the Tandy case is that most of its electronic products are manufactured in the United States, including all its desktop computers. Going against the conventional wisdom of the 1980s, when many companies moved production offshore, Tandy retained manufacturing close to home. The decision turned out to be correct when the dollar later dropped in value and the price of Asian electronics increased.

Let's examine Tandy's strategies:

1. Tandy management positioned Radio Shack as "America's Technology Store," selling batteries, recording tape, radio parts, cellular telephones, electronic toys, audio equipment—and computers. While half of retail sales come from products produced in its own plants, the remainder are high-margin name-brand consumer products from other manufacturers.

2. Tandy installed a computerized point-of-sale inventory control system. Results: Headquarters added efficiency, productivity, and profitability to its product mixes by organizing them by customer purchase patterns, offering the correct product at the right time, and targeting special product lines at the appropriate store locations. Also, the system permitted managers to scrutinize store operations with greater accuracy, deciding which stores to expand or to close.

3. Tandy managers applied shrewd business judgment, understanding which factors made the company successful, then knowing what to retain or change. Such judgment related to the stodgy Radio Shack image (management defines it as folksy). The image evolved because of the sometimes cluttered store layout, with wires, batteries, and ear phones alongside sophisticated laptop computers and camcorders. A judiciously applied facelift of its stores permitted merchandise to be arranged so that customers walking in for a battery wouldn't be intimidated by high-tech equipment.

4. Tandy gained a foothold in Europe by purchasing Victor and Micronic personal computer lines from Sweden's Datatronic AB. The move positioned Tandy on the European continent with some good products with which to launch an expansion while strategically keeping a low profile against the industry giants.

Guide to Marketing Strategy

What can be learned from the Tandy case about becoming a niche-market leader?

While the four strategies executed by Tandy contributed to its success, the overriding consideration was avoiding a direct confrontation with the industry giants. To do so, Tandy used a segmentation strategy. Let's examine *segmentation* as one strategy you can employ to solve a marketing problem.

The basic idea in applying a segmentation strategy is to avoid a direct attack against market leaders, instead going for an indirect approach against market segments and niches that are emerging, neglected, or poorly served. Segments are portions of total markets; niches are portions of segments. In practice, however, the terms are often used interchangeably. (The strategy concept of direct versus indirect approach is discussed in Chapter 8.)

Segmenting a market is based on the following categories:

- *Demographic:* Age, sex, family life cycle, race/ethnic/religious groups, education, income, occupation
- *Geographic:* Region, urban/suburban/rural, population density, city size, climate
- *Psychographic:* Life style, cultural values, psychological variables (personality, self-image)
- *Product factors:* Performance, quality, delivery, service, price

These categories are the most common approaches to segmentation. However, segments do not remain static. Wide interpretation and creativity can apply in identifying groups of individuals that have common needs and have buying power and that are measurable, accessible, and profitable.

In addition, consider the following guidelines for selecting a target segment:

- *Segment attractiveness.* Determine if the segment has the same degree of attractiveness, in terms of size and growth, to you as to your competitors. Is there enough room for growth among all rivals, or is there a threat of competitive warfare?
- *Segment structure.* Where does the buying power lie—with customers, distributors, or suppliers? Is there a threat of additional competitors coming into the segment because there are few entry barriers? Is there a threat of a substitute product or technology, for example, plastic replacing steel? Are ample quantities of resources (materials and people) available?
- *Segment objectives and resources.* What are the long-term objectives for the segment? What commitment—major, moderate, or low—

is your company willing to make to expand and/or defend the segment?

CASE EXAMPLE FOR MARKETING PROBLEM 4: HOW CAN YOU DIFFERENTIATE A COMMODITY PRODUCT AND REDUCE PRESSURE ON PRICE?

Georgia-Pacific Corporation is a prime example of a forest-products company. It was once anchored to commodity wood products and paper. Then, faced by a hostile economic and competitive environment, it shifted direction. Georgia-Pacific's hostile environment included changing buyer behavior, aggressive domestic competitors, industry consolidations, and new offshore competitors that attacked its traditional markets with low-priced, high-quality products.

Given those mind-jarring problems, Georgia-Pacific's managers responded with aggressive marketing strategies. The bottom line: Operating income from its pulp and paper division shot up twelvefold between 1985 and 1990 and earnings climbed steadily to an impressive 18 percent in a flat economy.

Let's examine four key components of Georgia-Pacific's strategy:

1. *Customer behavior:* With 141 wholesale outlets, Georgia-Pacific used its distribution network to watch customer buying patterns. It monitored professional builders and retail home improvement centers to view competitors' activities and gain valuable reaction time.

2. *Product development:* A Georgia-Pacific senior executive described product development as follows: "We look for intelligence from every major market. Then we can better meet the needs of the customers and find opportunities for value-added, higher-margin products."

3. *Organizational change:* Georgia-Pacific managers reacted to two market forces: remodeling as an alternative to new construction and a growing segment among do-it-yourselfers. They initiated organizational changes to match external market forces; for example, cost-cutting, plant modernization, and intensified market-driven planning resulted in a competitive advantage.

4. *Market expansion:* Georgia-Pacific managers identified opportunities in such markets as premium-branded tissues and towels. For example, Georgia-Pacific launched its brand AngelSoft in a highly

competitive market. In only eighteen months, it had grabbed an impressive 6 percent market share in the $2 billion market—excellent performance against such formidable competitors as Scott Paper Company and Procter & Gamble.

Guide to Marketing Strategy

Georgia-Pacific's managers resolved their products would be *differentiated*. Their strategy for achieving this goal offers pragmatic guidelines.

1. Make the major assumption that *all* products and services—even commodities—lend themselves to differentiation.
2. Study the areas of differentiation shown in Figure 9-1, which are derived from the marketing mix. If any areas meet customer needs and are superior to your competitors' level of performance, you could have a successful differentiation strategy.
3. Consider other differentiation approaches: providing technical support, offering financial advice and/or financial support, installing hot lines for immediate access to technical people or senior executives. The opportunities are open-ended.

ACTIVATING THE MARKETING MIX

The marketing mix is the dominant ingredient in strategy development, for it represents those areas in which the managers can exercise control. This section provides detail on activating each component of the marketing mix—for instance, introducing a new product design, developing a new pricing policy, launching a new promotional campaign, realigning the means of distribution, or perhaps combining all four components.

Product Strategies

A product may be defined as "a collection of benefits housed within a physical framework." The key word in that definition is "benefits." Unless a product has benefits in the eyes of the customer, it will not satisfy a customer need or want. How well a company can satisfy cus-

Figure 9-1. Areas of marketing differentiation.

- PRODUCT
  - Quality
  - Features
  - Options
  - Style
  - Brand name
  - Packaging
  - Sizes
  - Services
  - Warranties
  - Returns
  - Versatility
  - Uniqueness
  - Utility
  - Reliability
  - Durability
  - Guarantees

- PRICE
  - List price
  - Discounts
  - Allowances
  - Payment period
  - Credit terms

- DISTRIBUTION
  - Channels
  - Warranties
  - Direct sales force
  - Distributors
  - Dealers
  - Market coverage
  - Warehouse locations
  - Inventory control systems
  - Physical transport

- PROMOTION
  - Advertising
  - Customer promotion
  - Trade promotion
  - Personal selling incentives
  - Sales aids
  - Samples
  - Demonstrations
  - Contests
  - Premiums
  - Coupons
  - Manuals
  - Telemarketing
  - Publicity

tomer needs and wants, and do it at a reasonable profit, determines the success of that company.

If a company concentrates its marketing effort on a product, the action may involve launching a new product or strengthening sales of an existing product. Sometimes the action is planned to accomplish both jobs. For example, a new laptop computer can be promoted not only for its portable features but as a valuable addition to the line of office equipment that the company offers.

New Products. New products are the lifeblood of business growth and competitiveness. A company that eliminates new-product development and is content to stay with the same old product lines is vulnerable to being labeled out-of-step by industry standards and behind the times by customer perceptions. Yet the process of coming up with a need-satisfying and want-satisfying (and one hopes customer-satisfying and profitable) new product is becoming increasingly difficult. Between seven and nine of every ten products introduced over a given year do not become commercial successes. That sobering statistic means that careful planning must accompany every step of the marketing effort for a new product.

Good planning uses the organizational structure to the best advantage. The process involves thinking in terms of new products, following a careful procedure of generating and testing product ideas, and knowing when and how to launch a new product to give it the best chance of success.

Unfortunately, too many companies treat new-product development as a haphazard function, reacting to competitive efforts instead of planning: Company A brings out something that seems new and profitable, so Company B works out a variation of that product to get some of the market. Planning for new products should be an integral part of a company's organization.

A formal system that encourages the company to initiate action rather than simply react to what other companies produce should be set up. A widely used system of organizing for new-product development is the product-planning committee or the business management team. (The team approach is discussed in Chapter 6.) This team should have a formal status within the company organization. It should meet regularly and be expected to show results. The results within the strategic marketing planning process are identified in the business portfolio section of the plan.

If the company is a manufacturer, the team members should represent production, marketing, sales, technical, distribution, and finance. In a retailing company, the broad divisions of merchandise carried by the company might be represented. For companies in which technology is important, it is essential to have a research and development expert on the team, ideally one who is in direct contact with the marketplace and with the sales department. In those companies that handle large quantities of consumer goods, a product manager or brand manager is vital in pointing out where a new product might fit into the company's offerings.

The size of the team is not critical. Rather, it is the functions represented on the team that determine the quality of the outcomes. Further, to be productive the team needs full support of top management. And the team should be empowered to make decisions related to its strategic direction within the overall guidelines of the corporate mission.

Developing New Product Ideas. Once the organizational structure has been worked out, the team must set up its working procedures. The development of a new product begins with focus on the ultimate customer. The team's goal is to pinpoint a customer need or want and to seek out or develop a product that will satisfy it. The exact sequence of steps involved in such a system varies from company to company, but the steps that numerous companies use are as follows:

1. A steady flow of new product ideas is encouraged. This means opening up channels of communication with customers, salespeople, service personnel, and other company employees. New ideas also emerge through talking with executives at other distribution levels in the industry, meeting with the key people in trade associations, and keeping an eye out for what the competition is doing. The idea is to encourage people to talk about what they think is needed or wanted in the marketplace. Once people know there is an interested ear, they tend to report anything they think may be of value. Some of the techniques for opening the channels of communication include the following:

- *Customer visits.* Periodic visits by both marketing and nonmarketing members of the team open direct communication. Interestingly, some customers may be more candid with nonmarketing people, since they expect that there will be no direct relationship between their comment and service. Insight into customers' problems can be used to modify existing products and generate new ones.

- *Customer panels.* Selecting key customers from various market segments to form a panel provides ongoing information for generating new product ideas, determining level of service required, and monitoring product quality. It also serves as a source of intelligence about competitor activity. Such panels may exist at the distributor level and at the end-user stage.
- *Complaints analysis.* A common form of communication is the phone calls, letters, and returned merchandise from dissatisfied customers. However, studies reveal that 94 percent of customers don't send in formal complaints; they just go elsewhere to buy.
- *Surveys.* This form of communication varies from informal talks with customers immediately after a transaction to talks conducted at time intervals of six months to a year after purchase. More common are customer satisfaction studies highlighting the most common factors influencing customer satisfaction, which, in turn, serves as a benchmark by which to measure variations in each of the major factors periodically. The ongoing information is extremely valuable in maintaining lines of communication with the distribution network and end-use customers.

2. Given the flow of product and service ideas, the team must arrange a preliminary screening of those ideas. Obviously, only a few are likely to hold a real possibility. The rest are discarded or filed for future rescreening. Speed is important; although it is possible that too quick a screening can cause a possible winner to be lost, it is still better to discard even the "doubtfuls" and "possibles" and use the valuable time saved to focus on what seems to be a winning product idea.

3. Those ideas that pass the rough screening must be studied carefully. Here are some of the questions that must be considered:

- *What are the size and location of the potential market for the product?* Is there adequate demand to warrant its consideration? The size and scope of the market must be considered before anything else, for if an adequate potential market doesn't exist, it would be a waste of time to consider the problems of production, financing, and marketing.
- *Does the product fit into the company's present production facilities or*

product assortment? For instance, if a company sells office furniture directly to retail outlets, adding a line of imported desk accessories might complement the assortment salespeople could offer customers, but it would do nothing to help fill in slack periods on the production line. On the other hand, developing storage cabinets might increase the utilization of the production and marketing capabilities.

- *Should the product be manufactured by the company itself, or should it be purchased from another company for resale?* The costs and possible profit margins involved in the alternatives should be compared, taking into consideration the distribution timing as well. While this would seem a question only of concern to manufacturers, an increasing number of retailers now own or lease production facilities or source products directly from countries with low-cost labor.
- *How much financing would be needed?* A careful analysis of return on investment should be made, for this is the basic factor in determining the potential profitability of the product.
- *Are there any obstacles to securing a patent, if one is needed?* Can the product be designed to meet the applicable packaging, labeling, and quality standards?
- *Would the product help the company achieve its long-range objectives?* Decide—considering product-line depth, company image, market position, competitive advantage, and profitability—if the product, and the investment of money and human resources, will contribute to the organization's strategic objectives.

4. If the product idea still seems like a good one, it should be developed to the point where a limited quantity or a prototype can be tested on the market. If the results of the completed test prove discouraging, the company can still abandon the idea and charge the costs as a general expense of product planning.

If the tests are successful, however, the company should put its resources firmly behind making the new product a profitable part of its line. Because this step is so important, testing should be done in areas and with customers truly representative of the market as a whole. The testing should include not only the product; it should test the projected packaging, pricing, promotional theme, and method of distribution.

Launching a New Product. Launching a new product requires considering all the factors in the market environment. Some, remember, are controllable, and others are uncontrollable. For example, a company has control over its own marketing mix—the product itself, its pricing, its promotion, and its distribution. It cannot, however, control what customer attitudes and tastes are going to be, what legal and environmental restrictions may be adopted, or what the competition will do.

The biggest obstacle to any market is the competition. A competing manager has exactly the same choices in planning as does the manager of the company with the new product. The competing manager will try to unbalance the marketing mix surrounding the new product's introduction, attempting to keep that product from reaching its objectives, and will try to use as much effort to keep or lure customers away from that new product as the company will put into getting customers to buy the product.

The winner will be the company with the better marketing strategy. The company introducing the new product wants a strategy that will support the new product, one that will help the product quickly secure a good market position. It wants a strategy that will make it seem clear to competitors and customers alike that the new product is a formidable entry in the market, with uniqueness, benefits, and value.

Several types of basic strategies are used to launch a new product. The similarity among them is that each ties the new product, in one way or another, to the existing lines offered by the company. By doing this, the product adds strength to the total line and supports the corporate strategy. In three of the most basic strategies, the marketing effort is planned to underscore how the new product:

1. *Enhances the company's total product line.* The new product may expand the company's offerings by adding or complementing products already in the company's line. A bank adding a new service to its already existing line of services is using an expansion strategy. So is the supermarket that adds racks of small packaged toys to the lines it already carries.

The new product may also condense or simplify the company's lines. It may be a new product that replaces several older products, or it may be a new brand or category that replaces several brands or categories carried by the company. An electric blender that can chop ice, shred meat, and keep the mix warm is such a product.

2. *Is an improvement on an existing product.* One of the most successful strategies is introducing a new product as an improved version of what has been available. Usually the improvement is in the product itself—it lasts longer, performs better, does more. Sometimes, however, the improvement is in the packaging, the pricing, the promotion, or some other part of the marketing mix, particularly if the product is for a market in which there is a great deal of similarity among competing products. For example, a bank might establish new banking hours, staying open three nights a week or remaining open on Saturdays to attract people who are at work during regular banking hours. Such a move provides an added banking convenience, a definite plus for a promotional campaign.

While an improvement on an existing product or service doesn't allow the claims of uniqueness that can be made about a totally new product, it does link the past popularity of an old standby with the value of trying the new product. In a way, it extends the life cycle of a product by changing its marketing mix just enough to rekindle new interest.

3. *Helps the company project a new price image.* A price image involves trading up or trading down. "Trading up" means increasing the quality and average price of the product lines carried by the company; "trading down" means decreasing both the quality and the average price of those lines. There is some danger among companies that attempt to maintain a presence in the upscale end of the market while trading down by selling products at the low end. The danger is confusion in the mind of the buyer of what the company's position is in the marketplace.

Some Japanese car manufacturers have achieved success by serving both ends of the market without damage to their overall image. Once established with the low- and mid-priced cars, they carefully launched their upscale line of cars. However, they did so by establishing dedicated dealerships that made no reference to their lower-priced lines. General Motors, an American company, is a classic case of a company that spanned the price range of products, from Chevrolet to Cadillac.

Existing Products. With all the excitement generated by new products, remember that many existing products on the market may still be profitable best-sellers. Jell-O has been around since the 1930s, as has Scotch Brand tape. Nylon was introduced in the 1940s. Although there have been important new entries in the dessert, transparent tape, and synthetic fabric fields, these old faithfuls continue to produce substantial sales and profits for their companies. However, it isn't accidental that a few products happened to remain good sellers. The long sales life of these products results from carefully planned actions executed at specific stages in the products' life cycles.

Product Life Cycles. As we discussed in Chapter 8, the typical life cycle of a product follows a pattern of introduction, growth, maturity, decline, and phase-out. The order in which these stages occurs doesn't change, but the length of time a product takes to pass through each stage can be modified by the astute marketer. What managers have learned to do is to *extend* the length of the cycle.

When the product is in the introduction stage, there is generally a slow but gradual rise in the number of sales during the launch period. How sharply the sales line rises depends on how quickly the product becomes known, which in turn is the result of such factors as amount of promotional resources expended, efficiency of the sales force, acceptance by customers, and reactions from competitors. Price also has much to do with acceptance, for customers will try a lower-priced product more readily than a higher-priced product. As soon as a new product begins to build sales, the competition watches it closely, trying to determine whether it would be profitable for them to get into the market.

If the product is slated for success, it will show a sharp rise in the number of sales at the growth stage. This is normally the sharpest increase in sales found during the entire life cycle. At this point, the competition begins to pay close attention, ready to try for a share of business if the market looks promising. In addition, the first pressure from price-cutters and discounters begins to be felt, as the low-end marketers try to make profits on inexpensive copies. During the maturity phase of the product life cycle, the sales curve levels off but stays relatively firm. Quality product variations and refinements introduced by the competition make bids for the market, and price-cutting and discounting become more intense.

When the sales curve begins its downward turn, the product is in its stage of decline. Some companies pull out of the market completely, satisfied with whatever profits they have made. Other companies, even the higher-quality, prestige enterprises, begin to cut prices on what stock they have left in an effort to get rid of the inventory, or to eliminate their competition, in any way possible.

A product is usually phased out when it is no longer available in any outlet at any price; there is insufficient demand to make stocking the product worthwhile.

Extending the Life of a Product. During the maturity stage of a product's sales cycle, just prior to the decline stage, a manager has the option of getting out of the market or trying to extend the life of the product. Most companies follow the first course, turning their attention and resources to the development of a different product with a new life cycle. Some companies, however, develop a careful strategy that extends the maturity phase and delays the decline. This can produce a dramatic increase in the length of a product's life cycle and in the profits earned for the company. Here are four basic ways a company may be able to extend a product's life and thereby increase its return on investment:

1. *Promote more frequent usage among current users.* This means increasing the amount each customer buys. In three classic examples, Du Pont, once troubled by a trend toward bareleggedness, developed new lengths and better proportions for stockings to make them more readily acceptable to women; Jell-O went from "six delicious flavors" to well over a dozen flavors, encouraging shoppers to buy and serve in more variety; and 3M introduced tape dispensers for Scotch Brand Tape, as a regular part of the transparent tape purchase, making the tape easier to use and causing people to use it up more rapidly.

2. *Find new users for the market.* Du Pont tried to encourage increased use of stockings by teenagers and subteens, groups that usually stick to socks. Jell-O went after the weight-watching market. The 3M Company brought out both a lower-priced line to reach a new segment of the consumer market and a line of industrial tapes to attract commercial users.

3. *Find more uses for the product.* Du Pont added textures and colors to its available assortment of stockings, giving them sports appeal as well as dress appeal and encouraging the idea that it is fashionable to coordinate stocking colors with clothes. Jell-O showed cooks how to make salads as well as desserts out of its products. 3M brought out colored, patterned, waterproofed, and write-on tapes, which increased the versatility of their usefulness.

4. *Find new uses for the product's basic material.* Du Pont adapted nylon for use in wigs, tires, and rugs and for a host of other consumer

and industrial goods. Jell-O promoted its product's value as a health product—a fingernail toughener. The 3M Company turned out double-coated tapes, which competed with liquid adhesives, and reflecting color tapes, which competed with paint.

When sales of their products appeared to have passed through the maturity phase and were on the verge of a decline, all three companies did something to reverse the trend. Their actions were the result of careful planning efforts that had been going on since the introduction of each product. This planning enabled the companies to gauge when a change in marketing strategy should take place and to decide what the change should involve. As a result of product life cycle extension strategies, their products remain competitive and profitable in the marketplace.

Value Added. A concept related to product life cycle, value added is a somewhat different product strategy. It evolved as a response to competitors, particularly those from offshore areas with low-cost labor, who used low price as the primary weapon to capture market share. The value-added strategy assumes a total market-driven orientation of identifying and satisfying customer needs. Implementing the strategy means adding value to a basic commodity product and differentiating that product so that the added value overcomes and diffuses the price attack.

During the highly competitive 1980s, companies looking for innovative strategies to respond to price attacks began adding value to products by offering technical service, longer warranties, improved quality, just-in-time delivery, installation, and financial support, to name a few features. The source of these value-added features, for the most part, came from the marketing mix (see Figure 9-1).

An example of value added is demonstrated by Cargill, Inc. One division of this Minneapolis, Minnesota, conglomerate processes poultry. Responding to customer needs and to intense competition from organizations providing similar and sometimes indistinguishable products, Cargill moved away from a commodity type of business and adopted a value added strategy. For example, it now customizes packaging for department stores with food departments and for supermarkets interested in promoting their own private label. It also adds flavorings such as cajun, barbecue, or curry at the processing plant to appeal to a variety of ethnic markets and supplies major fast-food chains such as McDonald's with prepared chicken parts flavored and packaged to the customers' specifications.

Price-Planning Strategies

The second facet of the marketing mix is price. Price planning often involves answering questions such as, "What price should we charge?" "Should we go in with a high price, or are we better off starting with a low price?" "What can we logically and reasonably charge for this product?" and "Should we change the price, and if so, when and by how much?"

Answers to these questions are never easy to work out. However, decisions are more likely to be correct with an organized price-planning system that takes into consideration the company's objectives and present market conditions. The system should require that price decisions be based on the company's price objectives, an understanding of various price strategies, and, if necessary, a knowledge of how to combat price-cutting and discounting by competitors.

Price Objectives. Price objectives are essential. Well-stated objectives help dictate management decisions at all levels. If a pricing decision is in line with company objectives, then it has passed the test for whether it is the right move for a particular situation. The five basic pricing objectives used most frequently by companies specify that a company's prices should meet the following criteria:

1. *They should achieve a target return on investment or a specific net return on gross sales.* Return on investment is the more accurate figure and is used in many of the larger marketing-oriented companies. Return on investment, which takes into consideration all of the company's resources and how they are used, measures total costs against total profits.

2. *They should achieve market stabilization.* This is a type of "live and let live" policy, historically common in such major industries as oil, steel, and aluminum. The leading company in the industry usually sets the price pattern, and the smaller companies set their prices at or close to the leader's prices. Such pricing is legal and is not considered a form of "price-fixing" or a violation of pricing laws as long as the prices set are both justifiable and reasonable.

If the federal government does not consider a particular price increase in one of these major industries justifiable, it may threaten the industry with serious legal consequences, such as rolling back its prices.

3. *They should meet the competition.* Somewhat similar to the previous point, meeting the competition requires selecting prices that closely match those already being charged for similar products in the market. It is used in markets that are highly competitive as a means of keeping price-cutting or discounting from spreading and hurting all the companies involved. Instead of using price as a competitive weapon, some companies try to use product differentiation or value-added features, promotion, or distribution innovations to take pressure off price.

4. *They should maintain or improve the company's share of market.* This policy is used more frequently than any other, with the exception of the return-on-investment objective, and is particularly useful for companies that deal in very changeable markets. It involves setting prices according to what share of the market the company currently has and what share it wants to have, thereby using price as a major competitive weapon. Thus, it is the complete reverse of the "meet the competition" policy.

5. *They should maximize profits.* This price objective may sound like profiteering. Not so. Rather, it is a policy that views all the company's products as part of the total profit picture, taking a long-range approach to developing profits from those products. A company that plans in terms of maximizing profits may place a low price on a new product in an attempt to win a maximum number of customers for that product, on the assumption that those customers will continue to buy the product over a considerable period of time and thus create maximum profits for the product.

Pricing Strategies. A company's pricing objectives can and should serve as guides for establishing strategies.

Initial Price Strategies. When a new product is introduced and moves toward its competition, the company can use two pricing strategies: skim-the-cream and penetration pricing.

Skim-the-cream pricing is a strategy of setting a relatively high initial price on a product. The strategy often is used by companies that want to recover their initial investment quickly. It can be successful so long as the product is in the early stages of its life cycle and has a distinction that hasn't yet been challenged by the competition, for example, where the company has a patent on a new-product technology. The strategy is also used by companies that want to stretch out the growth stage of the product's life cycle and encourage the adoption of the product by those customers who are less sensitive to price.

Skim-the-cream pricing has one important built-in safety factor. If the price is set too high, it can be lowered, which is easier to do than raising the initial price of a product. The company prepares for this development by the tactic of step-down pricing or "cascading" the price downward.

Penetration pricing is the practice of selecting an initial price that is relatively low. Its object is to encourage as many sales as possible and to gain market share rapidly. The application of penetration pricing discourages competition, because other companies cannot figure out how to bring out a similar product at a similar low price, yet still make sufficient profit. This strategy has been immensely successful for companies from Japan, South Korea, Taiwan, Hong Kong, and Singapore in their initial approach to entering North American and European markets.

List Prices. In preparing the actual list price of a new product, a company needs to collect information about the market. Often this information comes from the development stage of the product; if not, it can be gathered from the salesforce or from distribution channels. Once the company has this information, it can calculate the list price. A company that introduces a single product at a time, such as an industrial equipment company, usually figures each new price individually; a company that frequently adds many products to its line, such as a department store, normally uses a predetermined mathematical formula, for example, adding a fixed markup over cost.

In preparing to set a list price, a company first estimates the probable demand for the product and the potential price range. These are determined by checking the prices and sales of competing products and by surveying wholesalers, retailers, and prospective customers. If possible, the product should be test-marketed to observe customers' reactions.

Next, the company must calculate how the competition will react to a particular price range. The major factor in any pricing situation is what the competition will do; a high initial price often encourages the competition to try to get a piece of the profit, whereas a low initial price may deter the competition from entering the market, at least during the product launch period. However, it is worth remembering the presence of three kinds of competition: direct competition from competitors with similar products, semidirect competition from companies making dissimilar products that nevertheless serve a similar function, and indirect competition from companies making completely different products that serve completely different purposes but that are competing for the same customer dollar. For instance, a company that manufactures oil burners is in direct competition with other manufacturers of oil burners and in semidirect competition with companies that make natural gas heating equipment. In addition, it faces indirect competition from companies that handle building materials or insulation supplies.

Finally, a company has to estimate the share of the market it wants the product to win within a specific time period. This is a key estimate and is the last step before figuring the actual list price. An aggressive company prepared to capture a large share of the market and with the resources to do so may choose penetration pricing; a company that wants to move relatively slowly because of the profile of target customers it wants to win or because it lacks sufficient product to serve a large share of the market may choose skim-the-cream pricing.

Alternative Pricing Strategies. Several types of pricing strategies are in use today. These include the single-price policy, the variable-price policy, price-lining, leader pricing, and psychological pricing.

The *single-price policy* means "one price for every customer, regardless of terms of purchase." It has the advantage of never being misunderstood by any customer or misunderstood by a regulatory agency on the lookout for pricing violations under existing or proposed legislation. On the other hand, the policy does allow a company to set varying prices based on quantity purchased in a single order, delivery time permitted, and other differences in terms of purchases, as long as the policy is used carefully within the limits proscribed by the law.

Price-lining involves concentrating the entire product offering within relatively few price lines, permitting depth assortment within a few price lines, instead of investing resources in many price lines. If a manager picks those price lines in which the competition is weak, price-lining can be a tool that concentrates a company's strength against the competition's weakness—an important characteristic of good strategy.

Leader pricing, which uses the indirect approach, consists of pricing one or more products low, using attractive price to draw customers who then buy other products that are priced for a higher return on investment. Leader pricing is a familiar policy of many lower- and medium-price retail stores, which use a special sale to bring in customers but expect those customers to be interested in buying other items at regular prices. Sometimes the bargain is even offered as a "loss leader," an item with a price lower than its cost, which in some areas is illegal.

Psychological pricing is the technique of making the prices sound right to the target customers. Sometimes it amounts to no more than a penny or two; stores that boast of their bargains usually use odd-figure prices, such as $49.97 or $49.98, whereas outlets that have a prestige image are likely to use round figures, such as $50. Odd-figure prices seem to suggest a special buy, whereas even-figure prices seem more dignified to customers.

Price-cutting can also be fought with nonprice weapons. Price is only one factor of the marketing mix; there are three other weapons, and a change in any one of them may make that important competitive difference:

1. *Look at the product itself.* Is there some way to differentiate the product to make it seem more attractive or more competitive? Is it feasible to increase warranty periods, offer money back if dissatisfied, or provide telephone "hot line" technical advice?

2. *Look at its promotion.* What about a new promotional theme, a fresh look to advertising, or the use of a different medium? What about premiums, or contests, or giveaways? Anything that can give new excitement to the product and add to its attractiveness in the eyes of the customer can help.

3. *Look at the distribution system.* Is there another way of packing or shipping the product that would be advantageous? Should different lines and channels of communication be considered? Can warehousing and order processing be made more efficient to provide, for example, just-in-time delivery?

Combating Price-Cutting and Discounting. What courses are open to a company when its competition hits the market with heavy discounting, excessive price cuts, and other price-war tactics? Before a company decides to join in the war, it should consider some alternatives. Admittedly, these alternatives are most likely to be successful in a fairly stable market. But even in a highly competitive market, a company faced with hard price competition should check the possibilities before starting down the road that usually damages profits for all companies concerned. Whenever possible, a company should try to meet competition, regardless of its type, not by countering with price-cutting, for price-cutting decreases profits, but by using all the other possible defenses first. Many nonprice strategies have been discussed earlier in this chapter, for example, using product differentiation, extending the product life cycle, or adding value to an offering.

Last Resorts. When all else fails and a company is faced with the necessity of joining the price-cutters, the move must work in the company's favor. Remember that:

- Off-season reductions hurt less than in-season reductions, because less volume is handled and there is a smaller loss of profit.
- Frequent price cuts on the same brand bring successively smaller gains in that brand's share of market, as the customer tends to lose confidence in it.
- Temporary price cuts seldom prevent new products from gaining a foothold in the market, for the effect of temporary price cuts is temporary itself.
- Price cuts on new brands are usually more effective than price cuts on established brands, for new brands are not as distinct in the minds of customers as the established brands.
- Price cuts seem to have little power to reverse a decline in the sales trend. When a product's life cycle enters its decline stage, all price cuts seem to do is indicate to customers that the product is on its way out. Some customers will continue to buy it, but more and more customers will be interested in whatever product is taking the old product's place.

Price-cutting is generally considered seriously by companies operating in markets with an elastic demand. But if the market is a steady, inelastic one, then price-cutting is usually ineffectual and results only in reduced volume and reduced profit.

Promotion Strategies

If a company has the right product at the right price, the next marketing job is to make sure that prospective customers learn about it. Promotion is a vital part of the marketing mix, the means of communicating news about the product and its price to those who will purchase that product at that price.

Virtually every category of product needs some kind of promotion in today's competitive marketplace. If the product is unique and radically new, that message should be promoted. On the other hand, if the product is just slightly different from others already on the market, then the promotion should concentrate on a particular claim that the competitor cannot duplicate.

Because customers are often bombarded by messages from various companies at the same time, it is important that the company tell its product story in a convincing way, in the right place, at the right time, and through the right combination of promotional ingredients. Working out how, where, and when the product story should be told is a matter of campaign strategy. That is what the promotion of a product is—a campaign. It is not a single effort but a series of coordinated efforts aimed at achieving a specific objective.

First, a campaign strategy should take into account all the promotional techniques available to the company, including advertising, direct mail, personal selling, publicity, and trade shows. Each method can be used in many ways; advertising, for instance, can involve the use of newspapers, magazines, radio, television, billboards, or brochures.

Next, the strategy must put the ingredients together in a way that has a synergistic effect; the combined impact of all elements of a promotional campaign creates a positive impact greater than the effect of each element taken separately. For instance, the famous slogan "Avis Tries Harder" would have had some impact if it simply had appeared in the company's advertising once or twice or three times, but the company chose to put synergy to work. For many years, it used the theme throughout its promotional campaign, plugging it in a wide variety of media, using it in everything from television advertising to lapel buttons. The result was that the total impact of one slogan used in various media had a far larger dollar-for-dollar value than it would have had the company used different themes in each medium.

The Promotional Mix. Selecting the right mix of promotional ingredients is a difficult job, for there are literally hundreds of possible combinations. Four factors influence the promotional mix decision: the budget, the nature of the market, the nature of the product, and the stage of its life cycle the product is in:

1. How big is the budget? For a small company with limited funds, the choice of promotional methods may be very simple. A small company may depend upon a few sales, a very limited advertising budget, and ample use of direct mail. A large company, however, that is willing to invest a large sum in promotion has more options as it decides which ingredients, in what proportion, will result in the best return on that investment.

The key point is that the company, small or large, looks on the promotional dollar as an investment similar to the investment in the machinery used to produce the item or the cost of the warehouse space used to store the item. The promotional expense should not be considered a current expenditure that must produce immediate results. Instead, it should be considered in terms of its overall contribution to the total profits and the entire life cycle of the product.

2. What is the nature of the market? A market can vary according to its geographic size; whether the customers come to the marketer or the marketer must send salespeople to the customers; and, in the latter case, whether the customers are clustered or scattered.

A market can be local, regional, national, or international. A local market may be covered adequately by personal selling or by a moderate amount of advertising in local media, but a combination of promotional inputs is needed to communicate news about a product to customers in a larger geographic area.

Whether customers are expected to come to the marketer's headquarters, as to a retailer's store, or whether the marketer sends salespeople to visit customers, as industrial marketers must, also affects the promotional mix. If customers routinely come to an outlet to do their purchasing, then the promotional mix should emphasize first bringing the customers into the outlet and then convincing them to buy. If the company goes to customers, the promotional emphasis is on getting the customer to permit a salesperson to visit.

The location of customers requiring visits also makes a difference. If customers are clustered in a small area, each salesperson can handle several calls a day. If the customers are scattered, a salesperson may have a day's traveling between one call and the next. In the first case, a company might put its promotional emphasis on personal selling; in the second, it might align an equal amount of media advertising and mail promotion with the personal selling effort.

3. What is the nature of the product? If the product is a branded convenience item, the promotional mix will likely emphasize advertising and the amount spent on personal selling will be just enough to hire individuals to take orders. If the product is a specialty or a service, the job of personal selling takes on major importance.

4. *What stage of its life cycle is the product in?* The promotional effort is most important in the early stages of the product's life cycle. The emphasis in the introduction and growth stages is on interesting the customer in the product; any means that encourages interest should get preference in the promotional mix. In the industrial market, both personal selling and trade advertising are important, whereas in the consumer market, advertising in mass media is essential.

Promotional efforts during the maturity phase usually concentrate on those ingredients that communicate to prospective customers the differences between one product and a competing one, where the item can be purchased, and any other differentiating factors that satisfy customers' needs and lead to purchase. As the product reaches the decline stage, the promotional effort usually shrinks to only a minimum of advertising, and the personal selling effort is switched to newer products.

Promotional Guidelines. Promotion is more art than science, given the diversity of market factors, changing customer behavior, the uncertainty of competitors' response to the company's efforts—and the ability of the company to execute the promotion with skill and efficiency. Nonetheless, for nonmarketers there are some informal, rather broad guidelines that should be considered. They are neither laws nor rules but observations based on past promotional experience. Here are three:

1. *Personal selling.* This promotional tool should be of major importance in situations where there is a concentrated grouping of customers or where the nature of the product requires demonstration or personal counseling. Automobiles and expensive industrial equipment, for instance, require an emphasis on personal selling technique or promotion, as do all kinds of services that require explanation rather than product identification.

2. *Advertising.* This should be the main ingredient in the promotional mixes for products that have wide appeal and are expected to have broad acceptance, such as many kinds of consumer products. No amount of advertising can sell a product that people do not want to

buy. However, when people are interested in purchasing an item, informative advertising can help them decide which of several competing products they will choose.

Advertising also helps to back up the personal selling method by preselling the product prior to sales calls. Its role in the industrial market is slightly different from its role in the consumer goods market; advertising in the industrial market is usually intended to presell a prospective customer prior to a salesperson's visit, whereas advertising in the consumer market is intended to bring the customer into the sales outlet.

3. *Other sales promotion methods.* Other techniques, such as display, sampling, videos, catalogs, coupons, seminars, telemarketing, and contests, all have their special uses. Display is important in most retail stores, particularly for products whose characteristics can be judged easily at the point of purchase or that are often bought on impulse. Sampling, coupons, and contests are usually used to encourage customer interest in a product. Catalogs and, increasingly, video presentations are useful for selling products whose purchase does not require a personal inspection by the customer. Seminars work well if expert demonstration is needed, if a new technology or concept must be introduced, or if a large group of individuals must be reached in the shortest possible time. Telemarketing also serves as a promotional tool to reach the maximum number of people in a short time. It is also quite suitable in selling situations where a recorded message is more convenient for the customer and more economical for the seller.

Distribution Strategies

Many companies achieve marketing success by improving their distributing systems. The following examples illustrate the application of distribution strategies:

- Procter & Gamble used satellite communications from its major customer, Wal-Mart Stores, to its own distribution centers. The electronic linkage provided daily sales data so that orders could be shipped automatically, resulting in just-in-time (JIT) delivery with near-perfect performance—a remarkable 99.6 percent on-time delivery record.

- Black & Decker used its channels of distribution to create cost efficiencies for its retail accounts. It combined shipments of complementary products for do-it-yourselfers with such items as door locks and decorative faucets to help retailers increase store sales volume.

▪ Mitsubishi Electric used an innovative distribution strategy to launch its large-screen TVs. Instead of using mass market distribution and going head-to-head against Sony with its 45,000 retail outlets, it focused on exclusive distribution through a small dealer network of about 3,300 storefronts. It then followed through by introducing its Three Diamond credit card, which offered buyers a preapproved credit line of $5,000. The tactic served to sustain a flow of traffic and of repeat purchases through that distribution channel.

These successes illustrate the variety of strategies that move goods through the channels of distribution and that serve as competitive weapons within a total marketing strategy. Managers can choose from the numerous possible distribution strategies if they know the routes a product can take from its source to the end user. The routes, known as channel levels, include the following:

▪ A zero-level (or direct) channel, used by manufacturers selling directly to an end user through door-to-door selling, mail/telephone ordering, or manufacturer-owned retail outlets
▪ A one-level channel, which has one intermediary, such as a retailer
▪ A two-level channel, which includes two intermediaries, such as a wholesaler selling to a retailer
▪ A three-level channel, consisting, for example, of a jobber, a wholesaler, and a retailer

Not only is it necessary to select the channel level, but this has to be done in the context of the product, for example, whether the product is standardized, customized, or perishable; the characteristics of the market; the frequency of purchase; the price level; the amount of service needed; and the availability of product. Once that information is sorted, then three potential strategies are available:

1. *Intensive distribution.* This strategy is used primarily by producers of mass-marketed convenience products such as cigarettes and chewing gum. Little or no service is needed, other than maintaining delivery and keeping the shelves stocked.

2. *Exclusive distribution.* As seen in the Mitsubishi example used

earlier in this section, this strategy limits the number of distributors and/or retail outlets that can, or are willing to, carry the specific product line, based on specific criteria such as geographic location, access to defined niches, financial strength, or service capabilities. As a result of the reduced number of distributors, there is greater interaction between producer and the outlets. Exclusive distribution is common with automobile dealerships, high-tech products, and certain designer-label apparel.

3. *Selective distribution.* Selective distribution is based on the ability of producers to provide customized products to targeted customer segments and of distributors to reach and service those customers and thereby sustain a finely tuned relationship. Selective distribution permits focused marketing efforts and provides extra support in the channel linkage from producer to distributor to end user.

Distribution Opportunities. Many companies simply follow the distribution patterns that have become traditional in their particular markets and never plan ways that might increase opportunities for innovation in their distribution methods.

For example, some of the large meat-packaging companies retained branch locations along railroad tracks long after refrigerated trucks, centralized buying, regional warehouses, and prepackaged meats had changed the entire logistics picture of the meat-packing business; marketers, when asked about possible distribution changes, answered, "Why should we bypass the wholesaler?" "Think of air express, when we're practically sitting on top of the railroad tracks?" or "Establish regional warehouses, with what that would do to our costs?"

On the other hand, consider those companies that have broken with traditional patterns. Merchandise is now prepackaged and shipped directly from manufacturer to retail store, often with the store's price labels already attached. Think, too, of the communication systems that link store to warehouse to manufacturer electronically, so that order processing is almost automatic. And think of the automated warehouses themselves, with conveyer systems that load and unload distant bins and shelves at the touch of a switch.

Cost of Distribution. Distribution expense, like that involved in product production and promotion, should be considered a long-term investment in the total profitability of the product during its entire life cycle. Distribution costs are generally divided into three groups:

1. *Operating costs*—costs of actually moving the goods, including packaging, transportation, loading, and unloading
2. *Possession costs*—those connected with warehousing, insurance, and inventory control
3. *Service costs*—the costs of processing orders, as well as the penalties paid when special shipments are required to get the product to the right place at the right time

Distribution Spending Strategy. Ideally, distribution innovations come from finding ways of circumventing existing patterns and discovering routes not previously used that are faster or more economical than existing ones. This means using the indirect approach, abandoning the expected and trying the unexpected. Here are some of the possibilities a company might explore:

- *Change mode of transportation.* Consider a faster way to get the product to market. Speed of delivery is often a deciding factor in the successful implementation of the total marketing strategy. Switching from rail to air transportation increases transportation costs but can result in reduced warehouse costs; it may also enable the company to secure a premium price because of its timeliness on the market. Or consider a slower, less expensive way, if the product is one whose time of arrival isn't critical. The water route is used profitably by many shippers of bulky, but relatively inexpensive, products.

- *Systematize ordering procedures.* This may mean hiring more clerical workers, establishing a toll-free "800" number or FAX number, or installing computerized systems such as electronic data interchange (EDI), which permits documents such as purchase orders to be sent from one company's computer to another's. It entails increased initial expense but also means gaining the ability to process more orders with greater speed and accuracy; such a system contributes to the much-touted strategy of providing just-in-time service. It can also reduce the need for warehouse inventory and probably reduce the number of sales lost because of processing mistakes. It may also allow the company to use the time saved to take advantage of slower but cheaper ways of getting the product into customers' hands.

- *Combine shipments.* Most transportation companies charge less for bulk shipments, and many manufacturers and wholesalers charge less per unit for large-quantity orders. Thus, there are cost advantages in pursuing bargain shipping rates whenever possible and refraining from placing orders (or making shipments) until quantities are large enough to earn a discount. Black & Decker used this approach, helping its retail customers increase store sales volume by combining shipments of complementary products.

- *Increase the number of warehouses.* This is a major logistic decision for a producer. By making this investment, a company can control the shipment of orders to customers, thus creating a competitive advantage. However, it may be possible to maximize geographical market coverage more rapidly without investing in building new warehouses by adding distributors with warehousing facilities. Under this scenario, various possibilities exist, such as creating joint relationships with key distributors in which financial and technology partnering permits both producer and distributor to benefit from the arrangement. Conversely, distributors with warehousing facilities may approach producers to finance the automation of systems in exchange for providing close proximity to a specific geographic market.

- *Automate the handling of the product.* Transportation and warehouse systems have the capacity to be partially or almost completely automated, enabling the product to be loaded, transported, unloaded, and stored more quickly and more efficiently, using fewer personnel.

- *Automate the inventory system.* This change involves an expense again, but it can pay off in better control of the product and, often, a lowered level of required inventory; the less money a company has to tie up in inventory, the more money it has available for investment in other segments of the operation. For example, Seminole Manufacturing Company, a garment maker, and Wal-Mart Stores formed a successful supplier-customer relationship that used automation to cut in half the delivery time for men's slacks. Wal-Mart was able to be better stocked in all sixty-four size and color combinations of Seminole's slacks, and sales of that item increased by 31 percent over a nine-month period.

THE GLOBAL MARKETPLACE

International markets present the great challenge of the 1990s, offering huge opportunities for companies to grow through global expansion beyond their traditional geographic base. Increasingly, the world is becoming a global marketplace; consequently, the responsibilities of all managers broaden to assume the additional dimensions of a global manager.

Expanded air routes, new forms of communication, and rapid changes in technology have made the world more accessible, with coalitions such as the European Economic Community (EEC) and guidelines such as the General Agreement on Tariffs and Trade (GATT) creating more favorable conditions for world trade by reducing tariffs and prices. The potential is vast. The twelve countries of the EC (Belgium, Denmark, France, Germany, Greece, Ireland, Italy, Luxembourg, the Netherlands, Portugal, Spain, and the United Kingdom) represent a total of over 350 million people and a potential market value of $4 trillion. And, then, there are the new opportunities emerging from those European countries formerly referred to as the Eastern bloc.

What is global marketing? How are international markets selected? What are the sources of information to get started in global marketing? Let's begin with an example of global marketing in action with the activities of one organization, Dow Chemical.

CASE EXAMPLE OF GLOBAL MARKETING — DOW CHEMICAL

Dow Chemical is a familiar sight in more than thirty countries, from the Philippines and Finland to Japan and Brazil. Almost half of this global company's 56,000 people are based outside the United States, and 55 percent of its almost $20 billion (1989) sales originate in other markets.

Behind the company's international growth is a global network. As early as the mid-1960s, Dow recognized that global success meant competing effectively in local markets. While it pursued worldwide economies of scale, the company also strived for close ties with customers. Local managers, often working in their native countries, adapted Dow products and strategies to their markets' particular requirements. Whether purifying water in Brazil or developing a joint venture in China, Dow answered each market's demands with a worldwide leader's resources. People, plants, and products linked to combine a local touch with a global perspective.

Making these connections brings substantial rewards. Dow's customers get new ideas, products, and technologies when and where they need them, at competitive prices. Dow often gains the benefits of leadership: lower costs and a faster, smoother entry into related businesses. A worldwide network helps Dow stay on top of new developments and cushions the impact of difficult conditions in any specific market or country.

Dow's Global Approach to a Product

Polycarbonate resins are used in a wide range of applications, including appliances and automotive, electronic, and medical equipment. With their outstanding ability to resist high temperatures, the resins are not only replacing wood, metal, and glass but other thermoplastics as well. Worldwide demand for the materials is expected to grow at a rate of 8 to 10 percent a year through the mid-1990s. To participate in this growth, Dow is advancing in all three of the world's major markets—Europe, Japan, and the United States. In 1988, the company started its second polycarbonate production line in the United States and announced plans to build a new facility in Europe.

Also in 1988, Dow signed an agreement with Sumitomo Chemical Company, Ltd., for the marketing and eventual production of polycarbonates in Japan through its subsidiary, Sumitomo Naugatuck Company, Ltd. The new alliance brings immediate access to the Japanese market and fosters a closer working relationship with manufacturers that use polycarbonates. It also offers Dow more opportunities to work with Japanese companies in developing new applications.

Other Alliances for Growth

Other joint ventures put products on the shelves of local stores and supermarkets. In Brazil, for example, Dow's subsidiary, DowBrands, Inc., has established a joint venture with Sanbra to market household cleaning products. On the other side of the world, the Lion Corporation, a major consumer products organization, is bringing Ziploc bags to Japanese consumers. A licensee, Shiseido Company Ltd., is developing the Japanese market for Yes detergent and stain remover.

In another example, Dow's subsidiary, Merrell Dow Pharmaceuticals, Inc., has applied a local, personalized perspective in Japan, the world's second-largest pharmaceutical market, through licensees and the acquisition of Funai. This entry strategy develops closer relationships with Japanese universities and medical professionals. As a result, both Merrell Dow and Funai products are enjoying increased success. Japanese sales of Probucol, a cholesterol-lowering agent, which already had the top position in the market, grew by more than 50 percent during one twelve-month period.

The Dow example illustrates the enormous possibilities of a well-executed global plan. Joint ventures, licenses, acquisitions, management contracts, and exporting are the typical entry strategies open to organizations ready to share in global marketing.

Selecting International Markets

Before you select one or more international markets as targets for a global strategy, you must clarify precisely what you want to accomplish. Use the following fifteen items as a guide:

1. To sell output of excess capacity
2. To secure additional markets that will help support a planned expansion in capacity, allowing fixed costs to be spread over a larger base and permitting operation at a more efficient level
3. To employ idle capital resources and generate an attractive return on them
4. To provide a global investment, risk, and revenue balance
5. To deploy underutilized management resources
6. To apply proven marketing skills in a broader geographic area
7. To combat domestic overseas competitors
8. To preempt competition moving into an emerging market
9. To follow your customers abroad to serve them in all their markets
10. To maintain and enlarge your existing presence in foreign markets
11. To reduce transportation costs or other marketing costs
12. To avoid the imposition of import duties or other trade barriers
13. To gain and secure access to raw materials or developing technology vital to your business
14. To obtain the competitive advantages inherent in substantially lower foreign labor costs
15. To participate and gain a share in global business opportunities and growth patterns

Wherever possible, quantify your objectives. If your company's prime reason for overseas marketing is to sell output from existing excess capacity, the level of underutilization should be measured. If you are considering exporting in order to expand your operation to a more efficient level, you can develop a schedule of different capacity levels and their corresponding costs. A similar approach to each of the challenges will result in a quantified objective.

However, avoid permitting projected short-term returns to dominate your thinking. You should also consider objectives relating to customers and competitors when thinking of long-term strategic outcomes that cannot be accurately quantified.

Screening International Markets

The screening process for overseas markets consists of eight steps:

1. *Identify the basic needs served by your product.* For example, while bicycles represent exercise and leisure items for most people in North America, in many European and Pacific Rim countries they serve as basic modes of transportation. In North America, features such as color, multiple-speed functions, and racing handles are important selling features; in other countries a sturdy frame, foot brakes, and a luggage rack are primary features.

Further, such labor-saving devices as automatic dish-washing and clothes-washing machines may be highly desirable in North America and in industrialized countries throughout the world. However, the availability of cheap labor and various cultural factors lessens the sales potential for those products in certain areas of the world, particularly less developed countries.

You should remain alert to rapidly changing economies. For example, Mexico's economy has grown rapidly over the last few years, resulting in high demand for labor-saving, high-tech products.

2. *Determine how the needs you have identified are currently being met in the target country.* Identify which products are currently on the market and determine if they are satisfactorily meeting your prospective customers' needs. Are these products of local manufacture or imported? What type of import restrictions are in force?

If you have had prior experience in a particular country, assemble information about these questions from your own records, from your import customers, and from other contacts in the target country. Also consider cultural diversity, economic conditions, and legal constraints.

In judging need satisfaction in an overseas market, be alert to the danger of applying your own standards of value rather than those of the host country. Make a conscious effort to view your product or service through the eyes of a prospective overseas buyer. What may be important and impressive product advantages to you may be irrelevant to the prospect.

3. *Look at indicators that reflect the likely market potential for your product.* For consumer goods, some market indicators are population and market growth, per capita income, and other such measures that correlate with purchases of your product. For industrial goods, suitable indicators may be the potential sales volume to the user industry, employment in that industry, level of technical skills, and the number of companies that are potential buyers.

4. *Look for geographic clusters that expedite expansion.* For example, you can gain access to an entire group of transnational markets by locating a facility in a member country. A plant in England gives access to many Western European countries. This consideration is particularly important given the new relationships and the elimination of trade barriers among those countries.

5. *Eliminate countries with insufficient potential.* In the first elimination round, screen out those countries with inadequate market potential so that you can focus sufficient resources in markets of greatest potential. Also eliminate countries whose economic growth is insufficient, whose politics are risky, or where available labor or natural resources are insufficient or too costly.

6. *Rank the remaining countries by their respective potential.* Since your company can hardly become active in many countries at once, this step facilitates your subsequent choice by spelling out the relative attractiveness of each country still under consideration.

7. *Eliminate from further consideration those countries whose barriers make entry either unprofitable or too risky.* Investment restrictions may prohibit a profitable investment in a manufacturing operation. Currency regulations may restrict the transfer of earnings from a potential subsidiary in a given country. If any of these or similar conditions apply, the business climate does not seem to justify a long-term commitment. It makes sense to concentrate your efforts where they will receive a warm reception.

8. *Select promising countries for the development of marketing strategies and marketing plans.* In the final screening of your overseas opportu-

nities, select the most suitable countries for further analysis. Only a very select number of candidate countries will be considered at this point for the development of marketing plans and strategies. The plans should include provisions for later expansion of your marketing thrust to related countries and a contingency plan should the country experience an unfavorable change in economic or political conditions.

If you are unable to do the screening of overseas markets, many research agencies and consultants are available to assist in the evaluation. Also, it may be advantageous to employ researchers located in the respective target countries to conduct primary research.

For More Information

The following suggestions are provided for those interested in more information on international marketing. Also check the additional resources noted in several parts of Chapter 3.

Among the sources of information are the following: the U.S. Department of Commerce Trade Lists, World Traders Data Report, Marketing Handbook, Commerce America, Overseas Business Reports, U.S. Trade Center Reports, and Export Market Guides; materials from the U.S. Departments of State, Treasury, and Agriculture, the trade promotion services of individual states, the commercial departments of the consulates of the respective foreign countries, bilateral chambers of commerce, the *Statistical Yearbook of the United Nations,* United Nations Industrial Development Organization, United Nations Development Program, Organization for Economic Cooperation and Development, the European Community, and International Monetary Fund; domestic and overseas banks; and trade journals and periodicals, such as *Business International* and *International Executive.*

If the published data available to you are inadequate or are not relevant, interviews with representatives of government agencies, consular services, international organizations, trade organizations, chambers of commerce, banks, and universities or with consultants may prove helpful.

Index